The Costa Rica Experience

SOLO TRAVELING AGAINST THE ODDS

KELLY MILLER

WANDERINK PUBLISHING

Book Cover by Kelly Miller

1st edition 2023

eBook ISBN: 979-8-9896584-1-1

Paperback ISBN: 979-8-9896584-4-2

"To COVID, the unexpected disruptor that turned our world upside down. In the chaos emerged an opportunity to embark on an unconventional journey that, otherwise, would not have been possible."

Contents

Introduction

Hello! Welcome to my book for solo traveling through Costa Rica!

Here is a little background information on me, Costa Rica, and my journey.

Growing up, I never had a huge desire to travel. My first flight wasn't until I was sixteen years old and it was to Washington, DC with my high school. Once I got to college, my desire to travel began to grow. In my Junior year, I had the urge to be an exchange student and signed up to live in Spain for a semester. I guess you could say that I traveled solo then, but that was just a flight. Once I was there, I was too afraid to travel anywhere else by myself. I did make some friends that made it possible for me to take a few trips while I was there, but I still have regrets about not doing more.

My mother was definitely the overprotective type that put the fear of God in me that someone was going to kidnap me or something else horrible would happen to me if I was alone. My brother and I rarely even got to play in our yard due to her fear of someone grabbing us and taking us away. My grandfather always jokingly tried to assure her that after ten minutes with either of us, they would give us back. For some reason, that still didn't reassure her. As I approached my twenties and thirties, my travel bug continued to grow, but I still struggled with the idea of doing it alone.

The first time that I truly traveled by myself was in 2015, when I was thirty-five years old. I was doing a mission trip for my church in India with a group of women for ten days. It was my first time going to Asia and I knew that I wanted to stay longer. The flight from the US to Asia is really long and I knew that I couldn't just spend a few days there. After India, I had plans to visit a friend in Singapore. My friend and I were scheduled to visit Bali for a few days and I would go solo to Thailand for five days.

Did I want to travel solo? Negative, Ghost Rider. I asked everyone I knew to go with me, but I couldn't get anyone to say yes. Oftentimes I'd return from a trip and the people who said no would eventually do the same trip soon after. I guess I started inspiring people to travel at a young age. This is around the time that I realized that if you keep waiting for someone to go with you, you may never go anywhere!

Before our trip to Bali, I had suggested to my friend that we should be on the same flight. Instead, she decided to book a different airline carrier. While I was in India, one of Bali's volcanoes erupted! Great timing, right?!? It wasn't anything major, but it was enough to disrupt flights. Her flight was canceled, and mine was not. Her airline told her that they couldn't rebook her for at least five to seven days due to how many flights were disrupted by the volcano. By then, I would have been long gone. I had the choice of trying to stay in Singapore with her for those days, even though I had no place to stay and Singapore is ridiculously expensive OR I could go to Bali by myself. Unexpectedly, I found myself traveling solo sooner than expected. Bali and Thailand were wonderful and it gave me the confidence that I needed so that I could travel on my own. In 2018, I traveled solo to Iceland to see the Northern Lights.

For those who don't know, Costa Rica is in Central America between Nicaragua and Panama. It is probably the most expensive country in

Central America thanks to American tourists and expats, along with other foreigners. I had visited Costa Rica one other time about ten years ago. It was ten days of paradise and bliss. The trip was split between La Fortuna and Guanacaste and was completely organized by a travel agency located in Costa Rica. Everything was all-inclusive and pretty fancy. Up until this trip, Costa Rica was still my number one vacation of all time. I knew that I always wanted to make it back. When I had the opportunity, I jumped at the chance to go back and I was lucky enough to be able to stay longer this time.

At the time when Covid began to spread and made its way over to the US, I lost my job along with many others in March 2020. I was a physical therapist living in Las Vegas and working in a home health setting. When we went into lockdown, there were not many patients that wanted people in their homes and, at that time, I completely understood. My home health agencies either didn't have any work for me or some even wanted me to supply my own Personal Protective Equipment that was on backorder with Amazon for at least two to three months out.

When restrictions started to ease, it was still difficult to find work. I started to apply for any job that I had even half the qualifications for to see if I would luck out. I didn't. Vegas took a big hit from the virus, being such a touristy town and the current state government not managing things very well. After a year of not working and a relationship traumatically falling apart, my depression hit an all-time high. It got to the point where I attempted to take my own life. Of course, I failed at the attempt, but I knew that I was wasting away in Vegas. I wasn't sure where to go or what to do. I thought to myself, if I stay here, I will still have all my expenses to pay for and that was slowly becoming harder to manage. I also thought, there are other places around the world that I could travel to that would have the same expenses or even cheaper. I could either be wasting away in Vegas or sitting on a beach somewhere with a cold drink in my hand with a tiny umbrella.

After some careful thought and a lot of prayers, I decided to embark on my travel journey. I wanted to travel for twelve months, outside of the US, and hit my bucket list as much as I could. I was forty years old, single, with no kids, and in decent health. I had seen many people in my past, especially family members, talk about traveling one day, but once that day came, they physically couldn't do it anymore. I didn't want that to be me. I wanted to write a different story, and this was my time to do it. My plan was to travel for the next twelve months in the hope that I would figure out my next chapter of life. By then, it would give Vegas and the rest of the world time to hopefully return to normal or at least a new normal. It was my own eat, pray, and love myself journey.

So, I packed up all my things and put most of my belongings in a storage unit. I packed up my car with whatever would fit, along with my dog, Lady, and we hit the road. We drove from Vegas to North Carolina in just over three days, around the first of May 2021. My hometown is close to Charlotte, NC, where all my family still resides. My family was going to look over Lady while I traveled, and Charlotte is a pretty good home base with a large international airport.

Enough about me, let's talk about Costa Rica and the book!

Obviously, by the title of the book, this is about solo traveling. Can anyone read this book and still get something out of it who isn't solo traveling? Absolutely! Any of the activities that I did or experienced can be shared with other people or just yourself. I decided to write this book to inspire others, mainly women, to be daring enough to travel alone. Why mainly women? Men don't typically have the same fears or mind-space that women have when it comes to traveling solo. As solo women, we have to worry about personal safety, the best modes of transportation, who to interact with and who to stay away from, and even concerns over the appropriate ways to dress. Ladies, it can be done. I have encountered many people throughout my travels that wish that they could do what I have done, and they tell me how much I have inspired them to go out and do it themselves. I never thought that I was the type of person that would inspire anyone, much less inspire someone to take a trip around the world by themselves. But if that is the case, I hope to inspire as many as possible to take this incredible journey. That is how the idea for the book was born.

Other than solo traveling, what else is this travelogue about? What will you find in this book? There is talk about nature, lots of hiking and waterfalls, the search for wildlife, the tours that I went on and those I didn't, local food, people, chocolate, coffee, long-distance date nights, Airbnbs, hotels, transportation, and the sleeplessness and restlessness that can come with all of it.

Who is this travelogue not for? Anyone who wants an experience with tons of paid tour guides or resort-style vacations with an unlimited budget. Yeah, you won't see that here. Any long-term trip can be very expensive. Since I was aiming to travel for a whole year, I had to make sure that I budgeted my money appropriately. There will be times that I splurge, like my all-inclusive birthday weekend, but you won't see that often. Even though surfing and camping are very popular in Costa Rica, those are two things that I am not good at and therefore skipped. There will be times in the book that I mention if a beach is good for surfers or not, but you won't hear me discuss the size of the swells.

My original plan was to pick places where I could observe and immerse myself with the local people and their culture. Costa Rica was at the top of my list. I knew that June and July were considered the rainy season in Costa Rica, but I also knew that you could get some of the best prices. So, you may hear me mention rain a few times (or a lot!). Since I was on a budget, I did all the planning myself. That is no easy task. For me, it felt like a full-time job with all the hours that went into researching and booking all the flights, cars, lodging, tours, etc.

I knew from my original trip that Costa Rica is basically divided up into rainforest and beaches, with some mountains in-between. I chose to split my time between La Fortuna and Guanacaste because it was the best of both worlds. La Fortuna has the Arenal Volcano and a lake with amazing hikes, waterfalls, and awesome adventures. Exploring the Guanacaste beaches gave me a chance to reflect and relax. On both trips, I chose to visit La Fortuna first to enjoy as many adventures as I could so that I would need to lay on a beach by the end of the trip since I couldn't move from all the physical activity. I squeezed Monteverde in because I am a huge coffee lover and it was a highly recommended escape from the heat and humidity.

I have had many people ask me where I did my research and how I chose the locations, lodging, restaurants, and activities. Two of my biggest platforms for research were Google and Facebook. Google is your friend. You can put in the search, "Best Places to Visit in Costa Rica," "Best Hot Springs in La Fortuna," or "Top Hikes in Costa Rica," for example, and you will have tons of answers at your fingertips. Your job is to look for consistency. There are seven blogs that say that La Fortuna is a must-see, but only one says that you have to visit San Jose. Go with the numbers. Three blogs that I found myself going back to often were:

- mytanfeet.com

- twoweeksincostarica.com

- puravidamoms.com

Facebook Groups are also another great way to find information. In the Facebook Search, type in "Costa Rica Travel Groups." You will find tons of people on there, just like you, searching for the best places to stay, eat, etc. As far as accommodations, there were times when Airbnb was not an option or they were charging way more than a hotel. There were also times when I wanted a different experience, like El Mangroove all-inclusive resort or Sangregado Lodge. I searched Tripadvisor often looking at reviews for different places. Two of my accommodations I found on a friend's Facebook page from where they tagged themselves and I wanted to go myself.

Other than all of that, another great way of finding things to do once you're there is to talk to a local. I got several great recommendations from locals that I didn't find in all my research. Most locals are very happy that you are visiting and love to help.

After spending about a month planning my trip to Costa Rica, my flight was scheduled for Memorial Day of 2021. This is where my story begins...

Now, if you are like me and like to see pictures along with words, I have created a website where you can access my photo gallery. If you choose, you can follow along and see what this country has to offer. On top of the gallery, the website will include maps, restaurants and activity recommendations, and more. You can check it out at solotravelchroni cles.com. To access the photo gallery, go to https://solotravelchronicle s.com/costa-rica/ and fill out the Member Sign Up Form. You will need your Order number and place of purchase to gain access.

Itinerary

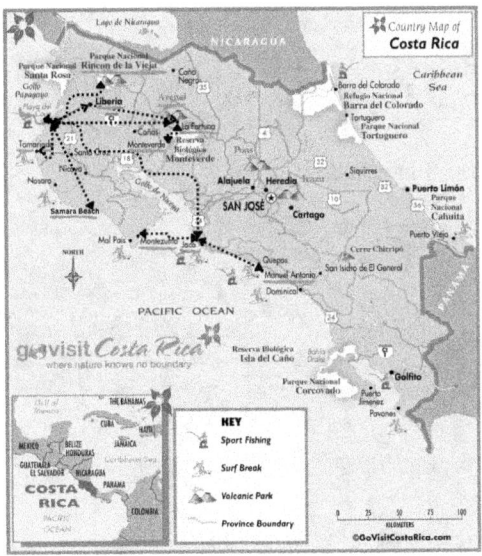

La Fortuna - 16 Days

- Arenal 1968 trail at the Arenal Volcano National Park

- La Fortuna Waterfall

- Tabacon Thermal Resort

- Don Juan Chocolates

- Rio Celeste and El Tenorio

- Venado Caves

- El Salto

- Chachagua Rainforest Resort

Monteverde - 7 Days

- Viento Fresco Waterfalls

- Finca Lluvias de Gloria

- Fallen fig tree

- El Tigre Waterfalls

- Bungalow at Sunset Hills

- Cafe de Monteverde plantation

- Kinkajou Night Walk

- Monteverde Cloud Forest Reserve

- San Lucas Tree House

La Fortuna - 9 Days

- Kayaking tour of Lake Arenal

Playas Del Coco - 15 Days

- La Leona Waterfall

- Marriott El Mangroove Hotel and Spa in Papagayo, Guanacaste

Samara Beach - 3 Days

- Exploring the Beach

- Ostional Refuge & Camaronal Beach

- Playa Carrillo

- Belen Waterfall

Flamingo and Tamarindo Beach - 1 Day

- Wabi Sabi

- Wild Panda

- El Chiringuito

Jaco Beach - 3 Days

- Cerro Pelado

- Exploring Jaco & its food

Montezuma Beach - 3 Days

- Zuma Boat Taxi

- Isla Tortuga Day Tour with Zuma Tours

- Montezuma Waterfall

- Dolphin Watching back to Jaco

Manuel Antonio - 3 Days

- El Mirador & El Miro Mountain - Jaco

- Manuel Antonio Reserve Park

- The Hidden Beach

- Back to Playas del Coco then US

Total= 59 Days

La Fortuna

Day One & Two: The Drive to La Fortuna & Arenal 1968 Trail

I arrived at Liberia Airport and got through immigration rather quickly. They encouraged social distancing, but no one seemed to care. I showed my Covid paperwork that was required to enter the country and went through to baggage claim. I had a hard time finding the rental car shuttle bus, my phone had absolutely no cell service in the airport and I was nervous as heck to practice my Spanish. It had been quite a few years since I had been anywhere where I had to speak Spanish. I finally found the shuttle bus and was taken to the car rental place. Car rentals in Costa Rica are crazy expensive due to their mandatory insurance. Even with my travel credit card covering the basic insurance, the mandatory insurance was double the price of the car. I used Adobe Rental Car and had a good experience. I packed all my luggage into my small sedan and started down the road.

The drive to La Fortuna takes about three hours, depending on how fast you drive, along with traffic. Most of the drive is down a long, windy, two-lane road, and you might get stuck behind a slow car for long periods of time. The drive is very scenic and crazy beautiful. At one point, you reach the top of some lookout points where you can see Lake Arenal. I reached the lookout points at sunset and it was postcard perfect. I arrived at my hotel where I'd be staying for the next two days, Sangregado Lodge.

The lodge is on the outskirts of La Fortuna at the top of a hill. My cabin was stunning with a modern feel. The bathroom had an amazing bathtub that I instantly fell in love with. I knew that I would be spending a good amount of time in there during my stay. One wall of the cabin had floor-to-ceiling windows with blinds that were mechanically operated. Even the bathroom had a huge window by the tub. Unfortunately, I arrived at night and would have to wait until the morning for the views!

I didn't sleep well that first night. The villa was so quiet, but the walls were thin and you could hear every creature that was outside. What kind of creatures, you may ask? Any kind that you can think of! I heard birds, frogs, crickets, cicadas, monkeys, and more! I felt like I was trying to sleep in a Rainforest Cafe. Since this wasn't something that I was used to, I had a hard time getting to sleep.

The next morning, I started the day with breakfast that was included in my accommodations. Sangregado Lodge does not have a restaurant but works with the Lost Iguana Resort a few minutes down the road. My breakfast usually consists of coffee and then more coffee with a side of coffee, but since I knew that I was going to be hiking, I thought that it would be a good idea to grab something with substance. I also rarely turn down anything that is free.

I ordered a typical Costa Rican breakfast consisting of gallo pinto, scrambled eggs, tortillas, and sour cream. *Gallo pinto* ("spotted rooster") is a Costa Rican spin on beans and rice. Everything was very tasty and fresh, especially their yummy coffee.

I decided to attempt the Arenal 1968 trail at the Arenal Volcano National Park. There are two trails that overlap each other, Lava Flow and Forest. Lava Flow is about two miles, while Forest is longer and more strenuous. I had read that it was three miles, but my Apple watch clocked it at a little over three and a half miles. I didn't know which trail I was going to do until I got there.

This is hands down one of the most beautiful hikes that I have ever done, and I have hiked in Thailand, Panama, and other places in Costa Rica, and even driven a snowmobile over a glacier in Iceland. I don't mention this to brag, but to show the depth of what I'm trying to describe. The trail itself is clean and well-kept. Within ten to fifteen minutes of hiking, you will begin to see the lava rock on all sides of the trail. This was my first time walking through a lava field and it was everything that I imagined. For those who haven't heard of this trail or even the volcano, Arenal volcano erupted in 1968 and destroyed multiple cities, killing around seventy people. This hike is what is left over from that eruption. You also walk very closely to the volcano, which is unbelievable and, in some ways, indescribable. The lava rock itself was gorgeous, with its rich black and charcoal gray colors, while giving contrast to the lush greenery surrounding the rocks. As you begin to climb, you see Lake Arenal and the volcano and get blown away by its beauty and majesty.

About an hour in, you reach what I would consider a little "peak." This is a flat landing, and you get a 360-degree view of all of Arenal. I had to just stand there for a few minutes in awe. None of my pictures could have really done it justice. The landing was quite large and could hold a large group of people, but I was lucky enough to have the whole place to myself. The peak of the volcano was resting within a large cloud, as it does so often, but I had a clear view of Lake Arenal. I could see the bright blue water that was miles away and that seemed so still and calm between the rolling hills that surrounded the lake. The rest of the 360-degree view was of the lavish foliage that went on for miles, covering the rolling hills and showing the majestic Costa Rican rainforest.

Soon after leaving the landing, the two trails split and you have to decide which direction you want to go. I felt pretty good at that point, so I decided to hike the Forest Trail. You are rarely on a flat surface and are grappling lava rocks up and down the trail. For the most part, I only saw lizards and one baby snake. I was happy that the baby snake wasn't poisonous and at a good distance to where I didn't feel the need to crawl out of my skin. Luckily, there wasn't much to jump out at me.

On my first trip to La Fortuna, we were on a guided hike and a baby eyelash viper had fallen from a tree and was lying on the trail. We were lucky to have had the guide with us because we would have stepped on the poor thing otherwise. That's when I learned that poisonous snakes are the deadliest when they are babies. After the guide informed us of this, he then asked me to hold a tree branch that he placed the baby snake on so that he could take a picture. After I popped my eyes back into my head, I reluctantly held the branch, which broke after a few seconds and we lost the snake. That would be the highest you would ever see this white girl jump. I kept my fingers crossed that I wouldn't encounter any unwanted creatures on this or any other hike while I was in Costa Rica.

Once you start to make your way through the Forest Trail, you get deeper into the rainforest and the nature sounds start to amplify. The insects buzzed just a little louder, the wind sounded more forceful through the trees, the frogs were serenading me just a little more, and the shrieking of the birds became more powerful. I felt like I was listening to a nature white noise machine in a surround sound theater room.

At the two-mile mark, I was starting to feel a little fatigued and was getting close to being ready to finish up the hike. Unfortunately, I didn't realize that I had another one and a half miles to go. Right when all the sounds were at their loudest, an ancient-looking staircase appeared and I felt that I had just been teleported into an *Indiana Jones* movie. You know the part where he stands there trying to figure out how that staircase just magically appeared and whether or not he should even climb it? Yeah, it had that kind of eerie feeling. I'm not going to lie, there was a part of the hike where I realized that I was completely alone in the middle of a rainforest. I couldn't hear any signs of human life and I had no idea how far I was into the trail. It did freak me out for a moment, but I just tried to keep calm and focus on the unbelievable moment of where I was and what I was seeing and experiencing. Then, at one point, I couldn't see anything and then the bushes started moving. I just looked at the bush and said, "Ok, you stay there and I'll go over here." Just wishful thinking that I had become a successful animal whisperer.

The last half mile or so, it began to rain. The rain felt so great and I loved the cold water hitting my skin, cooling me off since I was drenched with sweat. Luckily, the trees were giving me shelter from the downpour that was happening above me, so it was just enough sprinkle to cool me off. By the time I was finished, I was beat but felt amazing at the same time. Only my second time doing such a challenging hike and I loved almost every part of it. I recommend this hike to anyone.

After the hike, still drenched with sweat, I really needed to get a SIM card before Verizon emptied my bank account with all their extra fees. I drove into La Fortuna and found the Kolbi store. Kolbi is a government-owned cellular company, but they were still known to have the best coverage based on some of the blog posts that I had read.

Upon arrival, a security guard was standing at the door directing everyone to the bathroom to wash their hands. Afterward, she directs you to a chair and gives you a number. I literally felt like I was at the American DMV. Luckily, the line wasn't as long here. A woman behind plexiglass called my number and directed me to a chair in front of her desk, which was roped off to where my chair was about six feet from her. They don't joke about Covid around here! Plexiglass AND sitting six feet away. What is worse than a language barrier?!? Trying to hear and understand Spanish from someone wearing a mask, behind plexiglass, and six feet away. No pressure! Again, similar to the DMV, she was not happy to be working there and had even less patience for my Spanglish. I did get the SIM card, so mission accomplished. If you have never thought about a SIM card before, I would highly recommend one when traveling long-term in another country. I have used SIM cards in multiple countries and the cost is usually much more reasonable than what your local phone carrier will charge you. It will cost you less than twenty dollars for the month.

Since I was already in town, I decided to walk around and see what La Fortuna was like. It is not difficult to navigate the town, because it is very tiny, about eight commercial blocks. There is a very charming town square in the middle with a fountain and beautiful flowers and trees. There is also a gazebo where I saw some people sitting at a desk. As I got closer, I noticed a long line from the gazebo which went to the sidewalk and around the town square. It ended up being a line for the Covid vaccine. I had read in the media that Ticos didn't really want the vaccine. It is always enlightening to see for yourself how the media doesn't always give a clear picture from around the world.

I walked into some of the mini markets to see how pricing was going to be once I got to my Airbnb. In the produce section, I saw a vine of bananas that looked like the whole vine was cut and all the bananas were laid on the counter. There was even a *Crocodile Dundee* knife stuck in the vine, so people could cut off what bananas they wanted. I would love to see this in the States and see how many people would freak out over the knife just lying there or who would just steal it (lol). For some reason, I had thought that the prices in Costa Rica were cheaper than in the States, but was surprised when many of the prices were the same if not higher. I got a nice iced mocha from Chocolate Fusion. It seemed more like chocolate milk, but was refreshing either way since I was so hot from having to wear the mask outside.

I went back to my villa at the Sangregado Lodge and relaxed for a bit in the swing chair on their balcony. The skies had started to lighten throughout the day and had become pretty clear with a spectacular view of the Arenal Volcano miles away. I curled up in that huge chair with my laptop and a cup of coffee, and enjoyed my temporary heaven.

For dinner, I tried to find someplace close to the villa, because I had read that driving in the dark can be a little risky in Costa Rica, especially around La Fortuna. I could completely understand why as I had driven in the outskirts and witnessed the narrow and windy roads without any lighting around. I decided to eat at the Volcano Lodge Resort in their Sura Bistro, which I had read good reviews about in other blog posts. The resort staff were friendly and accommodating. I was trying to speak as much Spanish as I could but was feeling a little defeated and disappointed in myself at this point. I was fortunate that the staff didn't make me feel bad for not speaking the language perfectly. Their steaks looked very appetizing, but I wasn't super hungry. After taking a while with my indecisiveness, I decided on the grouper, but to my bad luck, they were out. I was tired of looking and settled on arroz con pollo (rice with chicken). It was very tasty, but I couldn't finish and took the rest of the food to the villa. I definitely wanted to come back to try more things on the menu.

Overall, it was a great first day.

Day Three: La Fortuna Waterfall & a Five-Pepper Steak

I slept really well last night, but was still awake at 6 am, ugh. Made some coffee and watched the view for a bit in the swing chair on the balcony, which I think has become my favorite spot in the room.

For breakfast I decided to try their huevos rancheros. I'm not a big fan of tomato sauce, but hot sauce makes just about everything taste better. The breakfast and coffee gave me enough energy to start another hike.

I arrived at the La Fortuna Waterfall, which is on the other side of the national park from where I was hiking yesterday at Arenal 1968. There isn't really hiking involved to get to the waterfall, buuuut you do have to go up and down five hundred steps.

The staircase zigzags down with handrails and landings. I didn't really have to take any breaks on the way down, but my calves were a little shaky the closer I got to the bottom. As you make your way down, you can slowly begin to see the waterfall appear through the trees. You will hear the water gushing down before you will see it. It's difficult to understand how big it truly is until you get up close to it. The waterfall is 70 meters (230 feet), or about 30 stories.

This is not your average waterfall. This waterfall plummets down into a gorgeous turquoise pool and you can see how strong the current is from a distance. People can swim in the pool but remain on the edges due to the strong current. The staff acts like lifeguards and will whistle at you if you attempt to go away from the edge toward the waterfall. This waterfall truly was a magnificent sight. I stood there for a few moments to try and save the mental image in my brain, took pictures, and sat down on a rock off to the side watching everyone enjoying the water.

Then came time to venture back up the stairs. I would say that it probably took me about fifteen to twenty minutes to make my way up the stairs. There were signs along the way letting you know how many stairs you had left. I'm sure that sign is there to motivate people, but as I was huffing and puffing and I saw the sign saying that I only went one hundred stairs, I was thinking, "You got to be kidding me!" Getting up to the top, I knew that my calves were definitely going to burn tomorrow and that I was so out of shape.

I went back to my villa and decided to relax there for the afternoon. I was a little tired and it was my last day at the villa, so I wanted to enjoy the quiet atmosphere and the view. Unfortunately, the property was doing construction work next to my villa. I tried taking a bath in their gorgeous tub and had music playing off my iPhone. Even with the volume on max, the construction was louder. Sitting out on the balcony was the same. Bummer!

I was craving steak and decided to go back to the Volcano Lodge to try their five-pepper steak. The same waiter from the night before was at the entrance as I arrived.

"Hello lady!" he said as he remembered me from the night before. His name was Jimmy and we had a lovely conversation most of the evening. They even had a happy hour from 4-7 pm: two glasses of wine for eight dollars. Not too shabby. My steak even came with a free glass of cabernet. The steak was great! I probably should have taken it off the skillet upon arrival, because it was a little overdone as I cut into it. It was still tender, juicy, and huge! I definitely got my money's worth and I still had one more glass of wine left from my happy hour deal.

I gave him my best smile and asked, "Is there any way that I could possibly take my last glass of wine to-go?" I may have even batted my eyes a few times just to hopefully add odds in my favor.

"Por supuesto! (Of course!)" he replied with a smile. He brought my third wine in a to-go cup and I knew that this was definitely my kind of place.

I started worrying a little about driving at night on my next adventure. If you have ever driven in the countryside in the South or New England in the States, it's about the same. There are a lot of curves, narrow roads, and no lights. You have to watch out for people who may not be as careful as you are coming around a bend. Your bright headlights get a great deal of action here at night, but otherwise, it hasn't been too bad .....yet. I will have to say, I have not approached an animal in the middle of the road coming around a curve. That might be a little different down the road (knocking on wood right now).

I was so exhausted that I went to bed around 8:30 pm. Wanted to be rested for the next day. Hoping to get to Rio Celeste. Let's see what happens!

Day Four: Rocky Start to the Morning, Tabacon Thermal Resort RNR

This morning I woke up at 6:30 am and felt great! Ready for the day. But wait ... I heard it pouring down rain. Apparently, it had rained most of the night and was going to rain most of the morning. I wasn't quite sure what to do. Most blog posts and reviews that I read suggested not attempting the hike if it had rained overnight due to being really slippery and muddy. I also read that there were multiple steep steps that you had to climb. As I walked around the room, I noticed that my calves were still pretty sore and they cramped up at the thought of climbing more steps. Back to the drawing board on what to do today.

I had to contact Verizon due to issues with my original SIM card. They wasted three hours of the morning to not fix the problem at all. I missed my last breakfast, missed a tour that I thought about going on and it left me scrambling to get all my stuff out of the room into the car by checkout time.

My Airbnb was nice enough to let me drop off my bags for storage until my room was ready. If you haven't read about it in other blogs or pages, it is not a good idea to leave anything inside of your vehicle, especially if you have a rental car. Costa Rica is a very safe country, but petty theft is their biggest crime. Many cars get broken into for even the smallest things left in the car.

Since Verizon and rain messed up most of my plans, I decided that I needed a spa day. When I say spa, I mean Costa Rican hot springs. During my first trip here, the travel agency had booked an evening of hot springs after one of our long hikes and it was glorious. Soaking your sore muscles in the natural hot springs is one of the best experiences. It is also said that these natural hot springs have healing properties. I'll take some of that! I booked an entrance ticket with lunch and dinner at Tabacon Thermal Resort. Upon arrival, they lost my reservation. That was just how my day was going, folks. Luckily, I showed them my email confirmation and they let me in. They tried to change my lunchtime and I tried not to be hangry, but my patience was getting a little thin. They honored my original time and I sat down to eat.

The food was great. I started with their ceviche, then my main course was a pan-seared sea bass. They wouldn't let you pick a dessert off the menu but served a little dessert trio instead that was still yummy. It was probably best that they gave me a small dessert because I was so stuffed from the other two courses!

After lunch, I went into the locker room to change into my bathing suit. I felt like a whale after eating all that food at lunch, but didn't care. I explored around and tested different hot springs on the property until I found a nice one all the way in the back that had some chaise lounge chairs nearby. Talk about relaxed; I ended up falling asleep on my stomach for almost an hour! Luckily, the sun wasn't that strong, so I wasn't well done upon waking. I ventured to the swim-up bar and ordered a coffee and coconut cocktail, which was extremely pricey, but very tasty. They even served it in a whole coconut after they took out the water for my drink. Even got a little umbrella in the drink too! Felt like Costa Rican paradise for a few moments at least.

Each of the hot springs had a different temperature that ranged from 77 to 122°F. There were twenty pools! Each pool was a different depth and there was a sign typically next to the spring entrance showing depth and temperature. Some were only one foot deep. Not too sure what the point of those would be, but maybe a nice wading pool for kids. Most of the time, I walked around with my flip-flops and went barefoot into the springs. There were a few that had natural bottoms with rock and sediment, where my water shoes might have felt a little more comfortable. I laid around until dinner, stopped off at the swim bar one more time, and then got dressed to go back to the restaurant.

Dinner was served at the same restaurant, and it had the same menu, but you could make different choices. I started with a salad and went for the chimichurri steak. The steak was perfectly cooked and tender. That chimichurri sauce was the bomb! Chimichurri sauce is of Argentinian origin and made up of red wine vinegar, garlic, olive oil, and parsley, but is found in many Latin cultures.

I got back to La Fortuna around 7:30 pm, just before it started to pour down rain again, and got to meet the senora of my Airbnb. My Airbnb was located in Barrio Pilo, which is in *el centro* (the center) of town, and it is the southernmost barrio before leaving town. The streets were very narrow and many people parked in the streets, which can make pulling in and out of a driveway difficult. They do not have traditional addresses like in the US or Europe. An address is about two sentences long and is pretty much a description of the house and how many houses you are from the nearest intersection. This made it very difficult when ordering delivery. I guess I'll be cooking or eating out while I'm here.

The department itself, what Ticos call apartments, was relatively nice compared to some of the homes I saw in the area. I never had a hot shower the whole time I was there, though. The owner made it seem that was normal for the area. I didn't really have any comparison other than the resorts.

I ended up crashing super early. Tomorrow, I'll be exploring and adulting! Yay!

Day Five: Adulting with a Weird Feria Experience

I didn't sleep too well last night due to it being the first night in the new Airbnb. I almost felt like I was still in the middle of the jungle with so many dogs howling and talking to each other all night, along with multiple birds running down my metal roof.

I had trouble sleeping almost every night because of the dogs.

There are dogs everywhere. Not just in Barrio Pilo, but all over La Fortuna. The majority of people own dogs in La Fortuna and many let them roam free. They let their dogs do whatever they want, including barking nonstop at all hours of the day and night. Walls in most homes are very thin, so you can hear everything. The times when it would pour down rain, which was daily while I was there, I had to wear my AirPods for Facetime or phone calls. I couldn't hear people, even with the sound on my laptop turned all the way up. The same for when the dogs were barking.

The coffee maker didn't put out much coffee this morning, so I had added getting coffee on my list, along with making a trip to a grocery store. Time to do a little adulting.

In La Fortuna, there are markets everywhere. There is a grocery store literally on every street corner, sometimes two on the same block. Each store can have completely different pricing. Just like in the States, there are small mini markets and there are supermarkets. Some days during the week there are also farmers markets, or *ferias*.

There was a Super Rosvil within a five-minute walking distance from my place. This market is larger and nicer than most mini markets you see in town. As in most places around, there was a hand washing station at the front door. After you washed your hands, an attendant standing at the door would take your temperature.

The store was clean, air-conditioned, and organized well. Right as you walk in you will see bakery items. That's always how they get you. I was really hungry when I got to the store (first mistake). I saw chocolate-covered coconut balls in the bakery section. I'm not going to lie, I ate one right there. It was like eating a Snickers bar in the commercials; my hangriness went away and I felt better. They were dang good, too.

They only had two jars of peanut butter, creamy and chunky. The jars were the smallest size of Jif that you could ever find in the States. One jar was almost $5.50. I had thought that peanut butter must not be a favorite amongst Ticos or just hard to bring into the country. I asked Ticos if peanut butter wasn't a thing here. They said it was, actually. I got some rice, coffee, olive oil, bread, sandwich meats, protein yogurt, mouthwash, and hand-wash laundry soap. My Airbnb didn't have a washing machine, so I would be doing laundry in the sink for a while. I may have left out one or two other things, but my total was forty-five dollars. I looked at what I bought and how much I spent and I had the same feeling that I normally get when I walk out of Target or Costco. Y'all know what I'm talking about.

I didn't get any veggies or meats, because the Senora of the Airbnb mentioned that there was a feria nearby every Friday, which happened to be across the street from Super Rosvil. I walked across the street to this little open area by a sports park. People had tables set up with veggies, meats, and small crafts. It's like a typical farmers market in the States, at a smaller scale.

I didn't have the best experience at this feria. Some of the produce looked somewhat small but expensive. One yellow onion, about half the size of the ones you find in Walmart or your local grocery, was one dollar. I know some of you may think, "Why is she having a problem with one small onion for a dollar?" Well, if you think about it, yellow onions are usually $0.99 or $1.50/pound in the states. Per pound, not one. Same for tomatoes. About one dollar each.

There was one seafood station that had whole fish, steaks, and filets, but it was all tilapia. Reasons why I don't like tilapia can be discussed on a different day, but I didn't realize how popular tilapia was in Costa Rica.

I found one table that had the largest green onion bunch that I had ever seen in my life. No joke. I thought that it came off of a farm from the land of giants and they looked scrumptious. I just had to buy one. I also saw cauliflower which looked pretty reasonable. One cauliflower and one green onion bunch cost me about two dollars, which isn't bad. Then my experience started to go a little off.

I realize that my Spanglish is very rusty and I had been trying to use it since I arrived in the country. There are many locals who are appreciative that you are trying to speak Spanish, even if it isn't good. I have seen tourists (mostly Americans) walking around and not even trying. When I say not even trying, I mean that they can't even say "gracias" as they walk away from a server, attendant, etc. There are also locals that really don't want to deal with tourists at all and get frustrated if your Spanish isn't top-notch.

I made sure what I was going to say before I approached the table. I am one of those people that will say the phrase at least five to ten times in my head before I say it out loud. Am I alone in this?? I hadn't been able to exchange any cash into colones yet, but I had read that many people will take US dollars. I asked a lady if she accepted dollars. My pronunciation of dolares (dollars) isn't always perfect, so I said it twice. She looked at me a little confused but then said, yes. I gave her a five and then she gave me change in colones. I could tell by her face that it wasn't something that she was used to, but it worked out.

I ventured over to the next produce table and asked two other ladies the same question. Those two freaked. I don't think they even listened to what I said and yelled for a guy a couple of tables over. Now, I was wearing a T-shirt that said "I like coffee and maybe 3 people" in English, buuut I was still speaking in Spanish. I must be a person who also needs to read lips because it can be difficult to understand and hear people with masks on. There have been times in the States that I have had to ask people to repeat what they said because of the stupid mask. Has anyone else had this same struggle since 2020? Anyhoo, the guy walked over and I believe he was American by his accent. He asked what I was asking about. I told him and he said, "Oh, they only take colones, but they don't speak English." I then told him that I spoke to them in Spanish and he just shook his head, shrugged his shoulder, and gave a slight grin. I don't think that was his first time encountering that.

Even though CR has a large expat population, I don't think some locals like dealing with tourists, at least from my experience. Unfortunately, CR relies heavily on tourism, especially from Americans. Like many other countries, CR was hit hard during the pandemic. As I was standing there with money in hand, I felt like Vivian from the movie *Pretty Woman*. I had money to spend, but people didn't want to talk to me or take my money. Boo.

At that same table was an American family buying produce. The parents looked like they were in their fifties. The man started talking to me in English about the States. It only took about two minutes into the convo for me to figure out he was a conspiracy theorist, automatically talking about how bad the country was getting with the current administration and that is why they moved to CR.

"Are you visiting or do you live here?" the man asked.

"I am visiting Costa Rica for two months," I replied.

"Well, I moved my family here, because the current US administration is so bad, there was no way that I was going to let my family go through that."

Not really knowing how to respond to that, I was able to muster, "Oh ok."

He then asked, "Did you take the vaccine?"

"Yes," I replied, "because I want to travel for a bit."

"Oh, that vaccine is going to kill you. It's going to kill everyone. Just wait until people start getting boosters," he said with confidence.

I then politely excused myself, saying that I had to find the *bano* (bathroom) lol. Even in another country, you can't get away from conspiracy theorists. I walked back to the grocery store to buy the produce that I was hoping for from the feria market and dropped it off at the Airbnb.

Other than Super Rosvil, on average, prices are higher than the States on most things. Cheap bread is over two dollars. The least expensive item that is also way cheaper than in the States ... coffee. Not only is the coffee cheap, but it's way better than Folgers or the other "budget" coffees. I could buy a pound of great-tasting coffee that was less than three dollars. True, I am in coffee central and the States have to import most, if not all, of it. I was happy about this, because, on average, I consume way more coffee than I do anything else besides water. As it should be. :) I am typically the person who always has to have creamer with my coffee, but I didn't see any creamer for coffee, other than milk. Luckily, the coffee tastes so good that I was able to drink it black.

Since the coffeemaker pooped out on me, I was still having coffee withdrawals. I haven't had much luck so far with the coffee places that I tried so far, including Arabigos Coffee House and Chocolate Fusion. After doing a little research, I found a place with good reviews called Red Frog Coffee Roasters. I decided to stop by after dropping off the groceries. The moment you walk in, a wave of roasted coffee bean aroma wafts across your nose, along with the smoke from the roaster. That mixture of heavenly aromas transported me to a countryside balcony overlooking coffee fields while sitting cozy in an oversized chair with a huge cup of joe. After jolting myself out of my daydream, I approached the back counter. I saw a small roaster where they were roasting the beans to order. I inhaled a little too much of the smoke from the roaster though. Whoa, that burned a little. Learned my lesson on that one. I ordered their house special iced coffee. That is some good coffee! Not watered down, just a little bit of milk with a whole bunch of tasty coffee goodness. As I was waiting for my iced coffee, that was my first time watching coffee being made from a chorreador, which is basically a sock or small sack hanging from a wooden post that serves as the filter for the water and grounds. Very cool to see! This might end up being my regular coffee place!

For dinner, I had read some reviews for a local soda that had really inexpensive, but good food. A "soda" is a local restaurant in Costa Rica, that is usually a mom-pop place and is open-aired. If you want basic, inexpensive, but traditional Costa Rican cuisine, a soda is the place to go. Soda Viquez was a seven-minute walk from my Airbnb. I got there around 5:30 pm and the place was mostly empty. That isn't always a good sign, but 5:30 pm is a little early and it is also off-season. The owner welcomed me and sat me at a table. She asked if I spoke Spanish and I said, "A little, but I'm trying." Her English was perfect. She asked how I found out about the place and thanked me for coming. The whole staff, which was mostly family, was very nice and hospitable.

I ordered a *casado de pescado*. Casado in Spanish means married. Not really sure why they call it this, other than there are so many different side dishes on the same plate, that they kind of combine with one another. Casado is a very traditional dish that consists of rice, beans, protein, and different veggies. The fish was sea bass. It was soooo good! I ate it super quick, almost too quick. They even offer some rice pudding or arroz con leche for dessert.

While I was eating, the owner's son came up and started talking with me. He tried to be patient with my Spanish, but did speak some English when he realized that there was something that I wasn't fully understanding. With taxes and everything included, the meal was $5.30! This made me rethink the whole cooking at home thing. I can't cook for this cheap and make anything quite that good! I think this was my day for finding my fave places in La Fortuna for the duration of my stay.

I'm glad that I had to walk home, because I was so full. It was nighttime but I felt very safe, and encountered many people who said hello and good evening in Spanish. Today I considered as a local day and looked forward to more like these. I haven't planned my day tomorrow, but a chocolate and coffee tour might be in my future!

Day Six: Day of Chocolate & Coffee with a Date Night

Was hoping to sleep in today, but it starts getting light out around 5 am. I can't seem to sleep past 6:30 am. I guess it helps me make the most of the day! At home, I usually walk about three miles or so every day. I realized that Red Frog Roasters is close to a three mile walk roundtrip. Perfect!

Between the humidity and the sporadic rainfall, I was pretty drenched by the time I got to the coffee shop. I'm sure they're used to that or at least I hope so! The staff inside is very friendly and enjoyed having a convo in English and in Spanish. I was enjoying my walk and coffee so much that I missed the turn to my Airbnb a few times!

Rain was off and on all day, which is typical of rainy season. I decided to do the Chocolate and Coffee tour at Don Juan Chocolates right outside of town. I attempted to walk there because Google Maps said it was a mile. I am realizing that sometimes Google Maps lies (lol). A mile and a half later, completely soaked, I was thirty minutes early for the tour. They said that I could enjoy free coffee before the tour began. Whaat?! I don't normally like being penalized for being early, but this time ... I will make an exception! Ha! Free is for me, especially when it's coffee. The coffee was excellent, too!

The tour started out with the chocolate-making process. They show you how the cacao plant is first started/planted, all the way up to production. It was so fascinating to me. One of the most interesting facts that I learned was that the cacao flower needs to be pollinated by a mosquito, so they plant banana trees and pineapple plants nearby to attract more mosquitos. Learn something new every day!

At first, it was just me and the guide, which I was enjoying. She asked, "Would you rather speak English or Spanish on the tour?" "Well, it isn't a bad idea to practice my Spanish, so let's do it!" I replied. After about fifteen to twenty minutes, an older mother and son joined the tour late. I didn't really get to practice my Spanish, because the son was adamant that the guide speak English for his mom. As we walked through the plantation, obviously we saw more and more mosquitos. The son forgot his bug spray, so I lent him some of mine. Just in case you were unaware, there are two things that you never leave your home in Costa Rica without: sunscreen and bug spray! Both are also expensive to buy here, so I tried to bring extra before I arrived. It is like liquid gold. He said thank you and that he owed me one.

We got to try and make our own chocolate. Making mine was fun, but you won't see me as a chocolatier any time soon. Mine tasted awful!! Luckily, they had some of their own for us to try. So much yummier! They even made us some homemade spicy hot chocolate. I love spicy, but I wasn't a huge fan. I think it was the texture of the drink because there were so many spices in it.

We didn't get to see many coffee plants because La Fortuna is not at the right altitude or elevation, but they still explained things well. They even had one of those small roasters that I saw in Red Frog that they roasted and ground some beans for us to try. They went into detail on how a chorreador works and how to use it. In Costa Rica, this is one of their traditional ways of making coffee. I had asked about the sock that was used as a filter and the guide said that many grandmothers still use actual socks today as the filter.

The process of making coffee through a chorreador is like a pour-over mixed with a French press. You take a pitcher of hot water and throw in the coffee grinds. After three minutes or so, depending on how strong you want your coffee, you pour it into the sock and press the grinds down with a spoon. It tasted ok, but she didn't measure the water or the grind, so I'm sure it could have been better.

There was a sign on the wall with some of the top coffee-consuming countries in order of rank. It blew me away. It was not the countries that I had thought of at all. The first one was Finland. Finland?! I had no idea. Columbia was #44. Yup, you read that correct, not #4, but #44. Whoa, mind blown.

The tour was over at around 5 pm or so. We could drink more coffee, but I didn't want to be up all night. La Fortuna is not exactly a place for nightlife, especially not during a pandemic. I decided to go ahead and walk to dinner.

My Google Maps said it was a nineteen-minute walk. I didn't think that would be too bad until it started pouring down rain five minutes in. As I was walking, I had to stop to let a car pass by that sprayed water on me like the beginning scenes of *Sex in the City*, where Carrie gets drenched by a bus. It was the mother and son from the tour. The son was driving. They saw me and kept driving. I guess that "owe ya one" didn't include offering a three-minute ride in the pouring rain. Oh well.

Luckily, I made it to the restaurant in twelve minutes; walking while soaking wet will speed you up a bit. I had more than two locals recommend Snapper's House to me, so I figured it would be good. My bf wanted to treat me to dinner from the States and it was going to be our date night. I know, sweet right?

It was about 5:30 pm again and I was the only one there. The server, Alberto, was very nice and was patient with me speaking Spanish/Spanglish. I ordered the octopus carpaccio and arroz puerto viejo. Both were excellent! I have never had octopus as a carpaccio, but it was thinly sliced and the cilantro sauce with what seemed like ponzu was so tasty. The arroz puerto viejo was rice cooked with coconut milk and sweet plantains, with a mix of seafood, including clams, mussels, shrimp, and crabs, that are sauteed in a tomato and calypso sauce. I don't usually like tomato sauces, but the tomato taste was light. The sauce itself was light and not overpowering and you could still taste the seafood well. The sweet coconut rice complimented the slight acidity of the seafood nicely; they balanced each other out. With those two dishes and two glasses of pinot grigio, my bill was around thirty-eight dollars after taxes and tip. Not bad for a date night out. How did it end up being a date night? We Facetimed at the table with my phone, since almost every restaurant has Wi-Fi. We both enjoyed dinner and wine two thousand miles apart. I was using my AirPods, so I wasn't that overly obnoxious person talking too loud on their phone at dinner. Sometimes you have to make the most out of long-distance, right? Many people have asked me how I have managed to keep a relationship alive throughout my solo travels. You have to stay patient and creative.

I have also had people ask me if I ever got funny looks while eating alone. To be honest, not that I have ever noticed. But I get why I was asked. It took me years before I was comfortable eating alone in a sit-down restaurant. I got a lot of stares in most places that I travel: I am a six-foot blonde, white girl walking around a Latin country, so eventually you just stop noticing or paying attention. I did see many other travelers eating alone in restaurants and I think that it has become a norm in most countries, especially in touristy ones.

No rain on my walk home. Just a nice night out with the humidity somewhat low for the area. Perfect night! Pura vida!

Day Seven: Rio Celeste & El Tenorio

Woke up this morning to a somewhat dry day. Since it didn't rain much Sunday and the forecast looked like it wasn't going to rain until the afternoon, I decided to venture up to see Rio Celeste and El Tenorio. The Tenorio Volcano National Park (Parque Nacional Volcán Tenorio) is about one and a half to two hours from La Fortuna. I made it in one hour and twenty minutes. The drive goes by pretty quickly. There are many more windy and narrow roads with large inclines and declines.

There were a few times I thought that my little four-cylinder Hyundai wasn't going to make it up the hill. I turned down the A/C and radio but thought I would have to start using my feet like *The Flintstones* on a few inclines. Many locals use the roads that lead up to the park and it seems that the speed limit and no passing signs are more like guidelines than laws. The last leg of the trip was on a paved road, but it had crazy potholes. If you aren't careful and on the lookout, you can easily leave an axle or your transmission behind in the street.

As I got close, I saw a guy standing at the edge of his driveway holding a large snake in his hands. The body was about the width of his forearms and probably as long as he was. I made sure to drive quickly past that house!

Once you reach the park, there is someone standing in the road that directs you to the right into a parking lot. The entrance to the park is across the street. The cost to park your car is two thousand colones or about three US dollars. There are a couple of guides that stand in the parking lot selling their services. I had read in a few places that it could easily be done self-guided, so I figured I would stick with that.

Again, they have you wash your hands before you pay at the entrance. The cost to enter was about thirteen dollars after tax. Very few people were wearing their masks on the trail. It was a somewhat strenuous hike, most would call it moderate. It would be a real struggle to try and wear a mask while hiking.

The hike itself is three and a half miles long. There is a map when you first enter, but it is not necessary after. There is plenty of signage that tells you where to go and how far everything is in meters. The first place you come up to is the waterfall (Catarata Del Toro). There are about 250 steps to go down with handrails and landings. I definitely took breaks on the way back up, but it was easier than La Fortuna Waterfall. This waterfall is just as gorgeous as that one, in the middle of a rock-walled cove. There was lush greenery and moss growing along the rocks with large, leafy trees that had branches that sloped down to where it almost looked like they were falling off the cliffs. The waterfall is 90 meters (295 feet) high and is a beautiful turquoise color similar to La Fortuna Waterfall, but lighter and brighter. You are not allowed to swim in this water, like at La Fortuna. Much of the water isn't safe to swim in due to volcanic activity from the surrounding volcanoes. There is a place down the street from the park that seemed safe enough to swim, since I saw many people down there swimming.

A butterfly/unknown bug flew past me and landed on a handrail. The wings looked exactly like leaves. It was crazy to look at! It's amazing the variety of wildlife and things you can see in this country that would be difficult to find in the States.

The next stop after the waterfall is the Mirador, or Lookout. It isn't far from the waterfall, but you have to climb quite a few steep stairs and scramble over some rocks to get there. At first, you think that you are just looking at some greenery until you notice the sign at about waist height. The lookout is where you have the best view of three volcanoes that are right beside each other. Similar to Arenal Volcano, it can be difficult to see a clear view due to clouds, especially during the rainy season.

As mentioned, the main reason I was waiting for a day with less rain to visit Rio Celeste was because I had read that the trail can become very muddy during the rainy season. The rainy season is a great time to visit Costa Rica, but you do have to be a little more flexible with your time due to the rain. The trail was muddy, but it wasn't bad at all. I had read some people having mud up past their ankles. The mud never got past the soles of my shoes, but my shoes definitely had to be washed after the hike was over. I did fall once and slipped twice, but no injuries to report!! Another reason to go when it hasn't rained too much is that the rain can cause sediment to fall into the river and make the river look brown or cloudy, and the blue of the water here is one of the reasons to visit. It can take a few hours for the river to turn blue again. Timing is everything during the rainy season!

After the Lookout, you will come to the Blue Lagoon, or Laguna Azul. You really get to see how remarkably blue the water is. Just to try and give a visual of how gorgeous it is, the color is so bright, it almost appears to look like a neon Tiffany & Co blue. The water was also so exceptionally still that you could only see movement along the rocks. Toward the end of the lagoon, you will see where the water turns from exquisite blue to being so clear that you see the river floor. A few moments after the water turns clear, you reach the Borbollones, or boiling water. You literally see the water bubbling. Some think that it is gas from the volcano, but you can feel the heat standing next to it and the sulfur smell was at its strongest here. There are signs everywhere that say not to get in or even get close to it! Can I get a hot tub?!?! Now that is one hot spring!

Toward the end of the trail, you will cross over two bridges; good stops to take photos of the water. It gets pretty clear at that point. At the very end of the trail, you will see where two rivers meet and what causes the water to be so blue. There is a sign there that explains the science behind what causes the water's color, and it is actually an optical illusion. They even describe the physics behind it or the optical phenomenon of Mie scattering. You see where one river is pure brown and a clear line between the brown and the blue water. It is truly remarkable.

The hike back was somewhat easier and felt much faster. In total, it took me about two and a half hours with stops. There weren't many people on the trail, and it felt as though I had the place to myself again. For the most part, when I am alone on these trails, I quite enjoy it. I love having the place to myself where I can hear the true sounds of the rainforest. Sometimes I would just stop, be still, and reflect on where I was and how I got there. Not logistically, but almost spiritually. Just standing there and taking in the whole experience and how blessed I was to be there.

Once I got back to La Fortuna, I realized that my Kolbi SIM card still was not acting right. My prepaid kept going down, but I had a monthly package. I was dreading going back to the Kolbi store. I tried to have everything that I wanted to say in Spanish on Google Translate. After looking at my account, the rep said something was wrong with my card/account. Yay.... They were going to send an email to try and fix the problem. I guess they don't have a tech support number. She said that she would call me with the solution. I never got a call.

Due to the number of calories I burned on the hike, I was hungry around 3 pm. I went back to Soda Viquez to get another casado. The owner's son and I spoke mostly Spanish the whole time. I was slowly gaining confidence in my Spanish. Don't get me wrong, my Spanish is still horrible, but it's slowly getting better. His name was Diego and he was friendly, and even gave me "locals-only" information. When I went to pay the check, he asked in English how long I was going to be in town and asked about what activities I had done since I arrived. He started to write down "hidden gems" that most people don't know about and aren't advertised on blogs and Tripadvisor. That was so nice of him! His list consisted of Venado Caves, Cerro Pelado trail, and Viento Fresco Waterfalls (heading to Monteverde). I couldn't wait to try some of his suggestions!

On my way home from the soda, I had a chocolate lab/pitbull mix follow me home. Obviously a stray, he was so cute! I couldn't tell at first, but I started noticing that he would walk a few steps ahead of me, and then cross in front of me to see where I was. He followed me for blocks, even when I turned down other streets and corners. I had my own little personal bodyguard and admirer. I was a little concerned that he would try to come into my Airbnb, but on the last block, another dog distracted him. I haven't seen him since, but it's a small town. I'm sure we'll meet again! Until then, good night!!

Day Eight: The Bat Cave & Back to Kolbi DMV

After taking Diego's advice from yesterday, I looked up Venado Caves on the official website. It definitely looked good and worth a visit. The website said twenty-eight dollars for the tour, gear, and access to their swimming pool. Google Maps said it would take approximately fifty minutes. When I woke up this morning, I saw that it wasn't supposed to rain until the afternoon, so I thought it was the perfect time to get in the car and head to the caves.

The drive is about half the drive you would take to get to Rio Celeste. You turn off Hwy 4 onto the narrowest road that I've ever seen. It is steep and windy. Close to the end of the road, out of nowhere, it goes from paved to unpaved gravel with major holes. I had to be really careful not to damage the rental car.

Driving down the driveway to the cave, I saw the pool off to the right. There was no water in it! I was worried if it was a sign of what to expect here. The website said that it was open every day, but I think my car was the only one there. When I got out of the car, I saw two gentlemen appear. When I started talking to them, they said that they didn't take credit cards and they wanted to charge me more because I was alone! Luckily, I had cash on me and they were charging me USD instead of colones, but I was already starting to have a bad taste in my mouth. I was able to talk them into not charging me extra because it wasn't mentioned on their website and the pool was also empty.

Once we got on the trail, my guide, Augusto, was funny; he made a lot of jokes and was very informative, making up for the bad introduction to the caves. He was willing to give the tour in English, but we decided that we would do Spanglish so that I could practice more.

Before we even reached the caves, he was able to spot a blue jeans dart frog. I thought he was pulling my leg with the name, but I looked it up, and sure enough, that was the name. For those who aren't aware of the frog, it is a very tiny frog. It may not even be as big as your big toe. I'm sure the guide is used to spotting them from a distance. They are bright in color with a red body and bright blue legs that make it look like they are wearing blue jeans. They are very bright, cute, and also very poisonous. The one thing that I learned in Costa Rica was the brighter the color of the frog, the more poisonous it is. We left that frog right where it was.

A couple of steps into the cave, and there was already a huge spider. I am not a fan of insects, especially big ones. It wasn't huge, but with legs, maybe three to four inches. That's big enough for me. It is very dark in the caves, but they give you helmets with flashlights on them and Augusto also had a flashlight on his wrist. You walk through water almost the entire time. The terrain in the water was rocky and I rarely walked over sand. I wore my water shoes, but you can also rent rain boots. Either would work. You just need something with good soles to keep yourself from slipping, because you will need the balance just going from one rock to another.

As you walk into the cave, the rainforest sounds that once surrounded you start to fade into silence. Complete silence, except for the occasional water drop and bat squeaking from up high.

We had to do a good bit of grappling up and down rocks. About a quarter of the way in, we reached a waterfall. Another advantage of visiting during the rainy season is that the waterfalls are at their best; much fuller and more beautiful than if you visited during the dry season. Right before the waterfall, Augusto pointed up and we could see multiple bats sleeping on the ceiling of the cave. Yup, they can stay right there, too. Let's move!

The waterfall was created from holes within the rocks of the cave and had multiple levels as it went down the wall. There was an opening through the waterfall, so we walked through and continued on our journey. We saw another spider along the wall that was three times the size of the first one. That thing was close to a foot. Not even joking. One foot! That was a big mofo.

During the tour, Augusto explained how part of the cave used to be part of the ocean. This blew me away because we were hours away from the closest beach. Not only that, we were so high in elevation! Some things are just so difficult to wrap your head around. He pointed out multiple places where there were seashells that were fossilized within the rocks and walls.

As we started to approach the back of the cave, we crawled through tight spaces and even crawled through water that was underneath rocks. This tour is definitely not for the claustrophobic. When the crawling was over, we got to another large area that had an undisturbed coral reef! I have never seen a coral reef out of water. It was mostly white and so beautiful. It made a slight staircase up several feet. Little pools of water formed on the tops of each "stair level." At the top, the coral reef seemed to intertwine with limestone. You can even see ripples in the coral/limestone. Truly incredible. Right behind the reef at the top is a large stalagmite. I'm pretty sure he told me what they called it, but all I could think looking at it was that it looked like Davy Jones from the *Pirates of the Caribbean* series. Tell me I'm wrong!

Augusto was nice enough to take my picture with the reef and Davy Jones. With just the right amount of light, the photo picked up all the colors that you couldn't see. Great picture!

We headed back the way we came, and Augusto pointed to a ladder off to the left side. Now it was time to climb. Once we got to the next level, there was a tiny space that we had to climb into. We were literally slithering on the ground/water. I could feel my helmet slightly skimming the rock above me.

We got to another open area with another huge stalagmite. He said that the name of this one was El Papaya. It did look like a papaya fruit. It was taller than me, and that's pretty tall. This is when Augusto told the story of the cave and how it was discovered. Back in 1942, a farmer was up above walking and somehow fell through the ground and down into the cave. Over the years, many people have broken pieces of the stalagmites and stalactites to take home as souvenirs. Kind of sad how people will destroy things just so they can have souvenirs.

As we crawled through more small spaces, we got to a place where we had to climb up rocks. As he went first, all I started to see were bats … SO MANY bats! Luckily, they were flying perpendicular to us, but I didn't think that they would ever stop coming.

Augusto kept saying "Let's go!" I said, "Where?" He pointed to the direction that the bats were flying toward. "Oh hell nah!!!!" I replied. We waited for a few more moments and he said, "That was the last one. Let's go." The moment we got up, more started flying by and one grazed my arm.

I screamed, "You lie!!!" I think I may have wetted my shorts at that point, not going to lie. I'm just glad there was a lot of water around and it wouldn't have made a difference.

As we walked, the smell of *guano* (bat crap) intensified. I was not happy about walking toward the smell or the bats. There was one more small space to get through and it was so small, I thought I was going to need butter to get through. My hips and shoulders were squeezed so tight. At this point, Augusto pointed upwards. I looked up. "Yeah?" He said, "We have to climb up the wall now." Um … At this point, I started having flashbacks from failing rope climbing in elementary and middle school. Luckily, he was nice enough to help me, and I was able to climb the wall. I actually felt a little good about myself, because that was the first time I had really climbed anything other than a ladder.

As we walked back up to the office, we got to talk a little more. He said that the pool is usually open on the weekends and he knew it was disappointing, especially since people usually have to drive to get there. Since he was so nice and helpful, when we got back, I gave him more money as a tip, more than what he originally asked for. My Apple watch said that I didn't move that much, but I told the watch that it lied. My body felt like I had done much more. I was spent, but it was totally worth it.

I was hungry by the time I got back and decided to go to a soda for something quick and cheap. I stopped back by Soda La Hormiga and grabbed a chicken casado. The chicken was fresh and tasted great. Definitely hit the spot. It was pouring down rain at this point and for some reason, I had the great idea to walk instead of drive. My phone still wasn't acting right, so I knew that I had to go back to the Kolbi store, which I was dreading—I didn't want to deal with this problem, and I didn't want to spoil such a great day.

I got there dripping wet and the security guard asked, "What do you want?" Yeah, pretty much like that. I said my phone, in Spanish, and he acted like he didn't know what I was saying. I said it again and he let me in. Even today, I was reading another blog post about how most Ticos in La Fortuna speak some English and they welcome English. Those bloggers must have never tried to get a SIM card to work in a Kolbi store. Legit. Before I walked into the store, I knew that I wouldn't be able to say everything I wanted to say in Spanish, so I wrote the whole paragraph in Google Translate and just handed the woman my phone. Think smarter, not harder, people.

I ended up in a forty-five-minute convo that was frustrating and did not go well. They were trying to say that I was making international texts with my phone. I was trying to tell them that I haven't been able to send an SMS since I got the card. The only texts that I had sent were iMessages and were over Wi-Fi. She must not have had much experience with iPhones, because she seemed a little confused by what I was saying. She was also confused because my phone does not separate what texts and calls you make with what number or SIM card. It also won't show if it was over Wi-Fi. She started pointing to texts that were used over Wi-Fi with my US SIM card. It's challenging enough having to fight with the customer service of a phone company, it's a whole other thing trying to do it in another language.

She finally got someone on the phone and I could hear her asking about iMessages. I could tell, because at this point she stopped and said, "Oh, como Facetime." She's getting it, folks!

She printed out a detailed list of the texts that were sent along with the number it was sent to. I don't even know what country that number was from! I told her that wasn't even a US number, because it didn't even start with +1. She grabbed my phone again and started to dial it in the phone section. I could tell that she was looking to see if I had the number saved, but I didn't. They put in a claim and asked if I could come back Friday. Oh yeah, the highlight of my day. (Insert sarcasm here). The only nice thing that I could say was that she did speak a little English and was trying to work with me so that we both could understand each other. I don't know how people do anything here without knowing a little Spanish, I just don't.

I was craving sweets, but I didn't want to go far for dinner. I found a place that was only a three minute walk from my Airbnb called Restaurante Cafe Mediterraneo. A super cute place with a wood-fired oven built into the wall, it had great wine, food, ambiance, and service. I noticed it was ranked #10 on Tripadvisor and I could see why. I wasn't hungry enough for pizza, but I definitely will be back for pizza. I ordered a pesto pasta that had avocado as one of the main ingredients. The pesto sauce was very good, but the warm avocado was a little weird. Warm avocado doesn't compliment the pesto for me. Since I was craving desserts and I like to try things that are different, I ordered their Baccio Arenal. Highly recommend it. They take pizza dough and wrap it up into a ball/knot. There is Nutella inside and they bake it in a wood-fired oven, then serve it with two scoops of vanilla ice cream on the side. Muy bien people, muy bien!!

I'm glad I walked home to make myself feel less guilty. Still, I've been here for over a week and there hasn't been one time where I have walked around in the dark and felt unsafe. Just a nice place to be and visit. I am full and exhausted. Off to bed I go!!

Days 9-15: A Local's Recommendation & Chachagua Rainforest Resort

Over the next few days, I was mostly lazy. I'm going to blame it on the rain. I did accomplish doing my first load of laundry by washing it in the kitchen sink. This sink was not that big and didn't have a stopper, so I ended up using a coffee mug and a bowl stacked on top of each other to try and get the water to fill up in the sink. The clothes seemed to smell cleaner, so I guess I was doing ok! The bathroom in my Airbnb was pretty big with tile flooring, so my clothes were hung up everywhere! The Airbnb host also had a drying rack outside, but it was a no-go on account of the endless rain.

On Thursday, I decided to get out of the house and go to a coffee shop for breakfast and do a bit of studying with my computer. I gave Arabigos Coffee another try. I just made sure not to order an iced coffee again. Upon sitting at a table, a young Tico by the name of Joshua greeted me. I asked him about the French press, or *frensa*. In English, he described four different Costa Rican coffees, along with their notes and aromas. I was very impressed. I tried the one that had chocolate notes and was from the more popular coffee region of Tarrazu, Costa Rica.

After choosing the type of bean, you pick your cup size: a six, twelve, or sixteen-ounce mug. I wasn't very impressed with that. You're paying for French press, but only getting a mug full. I ordered the sixteen ounce, not thinking that it takes me a bit to drink coffee and sure enough, the last

20 percent or so went to waste because it got cold and stale. The food was pretty yummy, however. I ordered avocado toast with a fried egg. The egg was perfect. Unfortunately, a hive of bees must have been creating a nest in the ceiling above me and they were harassing me throughout my meal.

Joshua moved me to another table, and I stayed for about two hours reading and doing stuff on the computer. Joshua would come over now and then to talk with me, asking where I was from, what I was studying, etc. I asked him in Spanish what he and other Ticos enjoyed doing when they were not working.

He said, "Most people in this area are always working. It is hard to afford living in this area because of the tourist prices, so most people have to work. When they are off, they will try and find free places to hang out with their friends and families." I really wanted to try and see what local life was like in La Fortuna and not just every touristy thing that I see on Facebook and Instagram.

He gave me a list of places to try and said that he would invite me the next time that he was going to one of them. I am not a person who can usually tell if a man is being nice or hitting on me ... eight out of ten times. This young man, the reason why I keep saying young man, must have only been twenty-five or twenty-six years old. I am not trying to be any cougar or Mrs. Robinson. I took it as he was trying to be nice to a foreigner since he knew that I was only in town for a short period of time. We exchanged numbers, and I went home to relax.

When I got home, I started to map out when I would try to attempt these "local" hangouts. The places he mentioned were El Salto (Rope Swing), a hidden trail next to La Fortuna Waterfall, and the free hot springs just a few meters from Tabacon Hot Springs.

The next day, after my morning walk, I saw that it wasn't going to rain until later in the afternoon. It was the perfect time to visit El Salto. I had the "local" directions: As you are heading out of town, you pass

Tiquicia Restaurante on your left. About a block or so after you pass the restaurant, you will come up onto a bridge that has graveled-out spaces along the side of the road where cars will be parked. If you cross the bridge, you will have gone too far. Along with cars being parked on the side of the road, there were two men who had a grill and canopy tent set up on the side of the road. They were selling skewers, or *pinchos*, along with drinks. The older man spoke English. He approached me while I was still in the car. Kind of creepy, but after a few minutes of talking to him, I realized that he was just being nice and trying to get business. He explained how the river works and what they were offering. He also pointed out some monkeys that were swinging in the trees overhead.

Walking along the side of the road, I noticed the dirt (mud that day) path that led into the trees. The path opened up to a rocky river with several levels and micro-waterfalls. There was conversation and laughter from those enjoying the river. Then, a Tarzan swinging higher up along the path. A group of kids were standing on the rocks, swinging from the rope and falling into the river. It looked like maybe a two or three meter drop. Nothing big, but it looked like everyone was having fun. Some people were lying out in the sun on the larger rocks. Most people seemed to know each other. It was nice to see a community within a large tourist town, similar to when I lived in Vegas. Huge tourist city, but locals knew where to go to be around other locals in their own community. I think living in Vegas and seeing past the stereotype of what Vegas represents is what fascinates me in seeing what local life is like in every town, and not just sticking to the landmarks and sights.

After hanging along the river for a bit, I started to get hungry and decided to venture over to Tiquicia Restaurante. It is ranked #1 on Tripadvisor and had numerous positive reviews. It is an open-air restaurant, like many in Costa Rica. It was so humid that day, so the moment I saw the word margarita, I knew it was a good choice. I ordered a passion fruit margarita. So delicious. I wasn't asked whether I wanted rocks or frozen, but frozen was what was delivered and I drank it. I couldn't tell, at first, if it had that much alcohol. By the time lunch was over and I got up to leave, I realized there was just enough (lol).

I like to try things that are different or unique to a place. They had a *pelea de gallos* (grilled sampler platter). It had Costa Rican roast, beef, chicken, and pork sausage. It was served with three tortillas and a salad and it was awesome. Everything was tender and had great flavors. The salad had cilantro, heart of palm, sprouts, just about everything you can think of to make a salad great with a little vinaigrette dressing. There was so much food that I had to ask for a *caja para llevar* (to-go box). The phrase "para llevar" came in pretty handy, which means 'to-go' in most Spanish-speaking countries. With tax and tip, the whole check came out to about $16.50. Not bad at all for everything that I got!

I didn't have time to visit the other two recommended local places before leaving for Monteverde for the week. I'll have to visit the others when I come back!

My Airbnb didn't have full availability for the month, so I had to stay somewhere else for two nights before heading to Monteverde. I made reservations at Chachagua Rainforest Resort for these remaining days, almost thirty minutes outside of La Fortuna. It was in the middle of the rainforest and so relaxing. I had a large bungalow with a huge bathroom. I took advantage of the bathroom to do more laundry before heading to Monteverde. I had to keep the bathroom door shut, because I think they had reflective material on the windows and birds were constantly running into the windows. Poor birds! My bungalow had a large porch with patio seats and a hammock. The resort itself was on many hot springs. I just spent the next two days relaxing, hot tubbing, and doing a little hiking. They had a few trails on the resort, but there wasn't really any signage and I thought that I had gotten lost at one point because I didn't see anybody on the trail for a long time.

I did get my first glimpse of an agouti, which is a small mammal that looks like an overgrown combination of a squirrel and a rabbit. Not as cute as you would think it would be, but they were all over the resort grounds. The property also has a small river and a waterfall that you can hike to. I then saw the largest ficus tree that I have ever seen to date. It was huge and had been there for over a hundred years. The resort was pricey, but I did enjoy my time and recommend a stay there. It's just too bad that it isn't really close to anything.

Monteverde

Day One: The Road Less Traveled

After breakfast around 10:30 am, I headed out of Chachagua Rainforest Resort to start my journey to Monteverde. I stopped for gas, which was about thirty-two dollars for seven gallons, and stopped at Red Frog Roasters to get my iced coffee. Then it was time to hit the road.

The weather was optimal: no rain in the forecast until the afternoon, as usual for this time of year. I dreaded getting back on Hwy 142 around the lake, but it turned out it wasn't bad. I think the last two weeks had given me a chance to get used to the traffic and going around the curves where I felt more comfortable. There wasn't a whole lot of traffic on the road, which was also a plus.

Following the advice of Diego (from Soda Viquez), I decided to stop at Viento Fresco Waterfalls, about an hour outside of Monteverde. It was easy to get to because there was plenty of signage starting about ten miles or so from the falls. The restaurant/reception building is off to the left upon arrival and the trail is to the right.

There was a nice, older man working behind the reception desk. He spoke relatively good English, but I had him explain things to me in Spanish (still trying to practice as much as possible). He showed me the map and the four waterfalls within the trail. I had already read in other blog posts that the driveway to get to the trail parking lot is uneven and unpaved. He also reiterated that it wasn't good for small sedans like mine and that I should walk it. He said that roundtrip, it should be about three kilometers, which is a little under two miles. Shouldn't be a problem.

It started to drizzle the last twenty minutes of my drive. I asked him if the rain would be an issue with the trail. He said that as long as it wasn't pouring, it should be ok. I asked for his advice on the right shoes to wear. I was wearing my Merrell hiking shoes, but I also pulled out my water shoes. He said that my hiking shoes should be good. I paid the seventeen dollar entrance fee and headed out. It had stopped raining as I entered the road to the trail. Off to the left of the road, there are lavishly green rolling hills with trees and bushes. Along the road, there were cows eating and watching as I walked along the path.

As I walked along this road, I could see why they recommended driving a 4×4. It is uneven and would have probably caused damage to my rental car. Because of the rain, the road was even starting to get slippery. I fell twice just trying to go down the road in my hiking shoes. This should have been my first sign that this hike might be rough today.

I got to the bottom of the road to where the parking lot was for the trail. When I looked at my Apple watch, it indicated that I had gone three-quarters of a mile so far. Along the trail, there are rubber handrails down one side. After going down a couple of flights, I realized that my hiking shoes were just not going to cut it. I sat down and switched to my water shoes. They didn't give as much support, but I had a better grip on the stairs and the trails. I couldn't wait to see the four waterfalls, and apparently there is a fifth that you can see from a distance. With approximately five hundred steps out and back to climb, I had read advice from others to descend all the way until the Slide Waterfall (the fourth) and then head back to the beginning while stopping to see the others. I thought that was pretty solid advice, and that is what I was attempting to follow. I saw the first waterfall off to the right side. Descending further, I reached a lookout point. To me, there wasn't much to see that I hadn't already seen, so I didn't stop at the lookout point. This is probably where I messed things up for myself.

I saw a sign pointing to the right toward the Hidden Waterfall. I somehow missed the sign that was to the far left showing that the Rainbow (third waterfall) was to the left. The trail was also slightly around the corner out of my sight. Somehow, I misread the map that was given to me and started to head toward the Hidden Waterfall. I reached the Hidden Waterfall, which is twenty meters (sixty-six feet). The fall is within a cove and has a cave off to each side of the falls. There are boulders and rocks that surround the falls, and they have another rubber railing that assists hikers over the rocks and across the river. Right here is where the mess-up began.

When I saw the sign near the falls that said exit, I thought that meant that I was heading back to the beginning. I also saw an additional trail past the falls with rubber rails, so I thought that the trail continued there. The trail then split off into two directions. One circled back around to the falls and the other went up until I reached a fence with a gate. I had read how another trail near La Fortuna has gates in order to keep cows from going in, so I thought that I was on the right path. As I went through the gate, I saw more of the trail with rubber handrails. I thought I was still on the right trail.

The trail had more stone steps, along with a dirt trail. Because of the rain, much of the trail had become muddy. If it wasn't for the rubber rails, there would probably have been many times when I would have slipped or fallen. Walking on this trail, I was fully submerged in the rainforest, completely surrounded by trees, plants, and shrubbery. Every once in a while, I saw a break between the trees to the green hills in the distance. On top of being surrounded by greenery, there is also another fully immersive surround sound nature show, with more buzzing insects, especially cicadas, serenading with their chirping. Occasionally, one would jump across the path right in front of me to help keep me awake and on my toes. I could hear hundreds of birds chirping and even monkeys screaming or howling in the distance. Yet, the majority of the time, I didn't see any of them. Occasionally, a lizard or two would wait in the bushes for me to get closer as they then decided to sprint out across the path, causing a potential trip or slide in the mud as I attempted to avoid squishing them.

Only once during this hike did I see another couple. They were close to the first waterfall. Other than that, I was completely alone on this trail. This isn't foreign to me. I have been on other trails here in Costa Rica where I have been alone because it's off-season. There are times when I felt a little uneasy about that. Around this time, when I started to feel that I might be on the wrong path, I became a bit more uneasy and also worried. There is no internet or phone reception. If I were to fall or get bitten by something, I would have been there for a looong time before someone would notice. I have done many things in my life on my own, but doing things like this can be a little more nerve-racking. I prayed multiple times for safety. Every once in a while, I started talking to myself, giving myself a pep talk to keep going and some reassurance that I would be ok.

This trail was strenuous with a lot of up-and-down climbing. Keeping my heart rate below 160 was difficult. Plants were beginning to creep into the trail and I had to step over or walk through them.

After a few hundred meters, I came to a split in the trail. Again, there was no signage, but I figured it was the two trails to Rainbow and Slide waterfalls. I took my chances and went to the right. After many, many steps, I finally reached a waterfall. From most pictures I saw online, I believed it to be the Slide waterfall. The waterfall looked just like the name. The water just slides down the rock along the side of the mountain. After a few levels, it ends down in a small pool for people to swim in. The waterfall is 95 meters (312 feet) tall. There is another small waterfall off to the left where there is another rock embedded in the terrain.

The cool mist from the waterfall felt refreshing after the hike to get there. I couldn't even really see where the normal part of the trail would have come out at. At this point, I still wasn't completely sure, but I thought that I was on the right track. I rested for a few minutes there and then headed back up the steps/trail.

I came back to the trail split and went down the other trail. I could tell that it was shorter because the sound of the waterfall was already pretty close. With more steps and muddy trails, I reached the Rainbow Waterfall. As I got closer, the waterfall was so strong, the wind that the falls created could have almost pushed me over. Again, the cool wind was welcomed. It was stunning. I had read posts from people who said they believed that this is more beautiful than La Fortuna or Rio Celeste. I don't think that I necessarily agree, but we all have different characteristics that we like to see in waterfalls that make them beautiful to us. It was magnificent and taller, standing at 75 meters (247 feet), but the area didn't quite have as much character and scenery for me as the other two.

A bonus was that there is a pool at the end that people can swim in. Across from the pool, I saw a small table with chairs, along with a staircase that went back up from the falls. At this moment, I started thinking that there may be more than one trail and I may not have been on the right one. Either way, I was almost done, so no biggie.

I retraced my steps and came back to the Hidden Waterfall. I climbed the steps back up to the Lookout and sat down to rest and get my heart rate down. As I sat at the tables and looked out, that is when I finally saw the Rainbow Waterfall sign to the left and the small trail rounding the corner. A "you're an idiot" lightbulb went off. Not completely sure how I missed that sign before, but I made it through, so it didn't matter now. Lesson learned, however; I now do a 360 when I hike to make sure I look for every possible sign.

It started to rain as I was trekking back along the driveway to get to my car. The driveway felt steeper going up compared to when I was going down. As I got in my car, the nice, older man came to my window and asked, "Is everything ok?"

"Esta bien," I was able to get out between the gasps of air from being so winded. I definitely wasn't going to tell him that I got a little off track. I took a look at my watch. Instead of 1.86 miles and 600 feet of elevation, I hiked 3.6 miles and 1,262 feet in elevation. I got my steps in for the day, lol.

I headed out from the Falls to get to my next Airbnb destination, Finca Lluvias de Gloria, which is about twenty minutes outside of Santa Elena from Monteverde. Part of the drive was a little stressful because it was unpaved and uneven. At one point, because of the rain, I thought that I was going to get stuck on an incline. More praying was involved at this point. I finally made it to the finca, exhausted and really hungry.

Upon arrival, the first person I encountered was the owner Hermida, a very nice, energetic, and feisty lady who is hospitable and loves to host others. One of the first things that I noticed upon meeting her was her Spanish. She doesn't speak any English, but the way she enunciates her words is perfect. I could understand close to 85 percent of everything she said, even with a mask on. I haven't encountered that since I arrived in Costa Rica. It calmed my nerves once I got there.

She showed me around and took me to Casa #1 where I would be staying. She asked if I was hungry and she had her granddaughter bring me dinner about twenty minutes later. She brought a tasty pork casado, along with eggs and fresh fruit from the farm. She also brought plenty of coffee, and I knew I booked the right place. As I looked around the casa,

I noticed the coffeemaker. It was a chorreador, the sock coffeemaker. I would get to try out my skills firsthand. This should be interesting.

I ate my food and crashed early. I knew I was going to be sore in the morning, but luckily, I didn't have major plans, so I could play it by ear. I'll see what trouble I can get into tomorrow. Night!

Day Two & Three: My Days as a Townie

I had trouble sleeping last night and woke up early. Before I went to sleep, there were so many bugs and insects that came into the room because of the lights. One even dive-bombed my face while I was on Facetime. It freaked me out to think they were lying on me to the point where I couldn't sleep.

I went to the main house on the farm for breakfast. Swatty (Hermida's granddaughter) and Hermida gave me a warm welcome and coffee right away. They gave me a few options for breakfast, but I think I was still carb deprived from the difficult trek at Viento Fresco Waterfall because banana pancakes sounded incredible. They were exactly that, incredible! They were some of the best pancakes that I have ever had, and they hit the spot.

I was talking with Swatty, and she informed me that they give tours of the farm and coffee making. We scheduled to do the tour in an hour to give me time to shower. Unfortunately, I got in the shower and it was ice cold. Not slightly warm or slightly cool. Ice cold. I made sure to get the important goods cleaned and I immediately jumped out. After the shower, it started raining early. At this point, it was only 9:30 am, which was early for rain that time of year. I waited for about an hour, but it wasn't letting up. Swatty and I decided to put the tour on hold until the next day.

I spoke with Swatty for a few minutes after breakfast. She was sixteen years old and attending school in Monteverde. I was unaware of this until I arrived in Monteverde, but Monteverde was founded by Quakers from the US back in the 1950s. They fled the States in order to avoid being drafted into the Korean War. They inhabited this part of Costa Rica and started farming the land. They saved a good portion of the forest, which became part of the Forest Reserve in the 1970s. Monteverde still has a strong Quaker influence and presence. Swatty has actually attended a Quaker school since she was four. That is also when she started learning English. She said that most of her teachers are Americans. She hopes to one day study English Literature and go to law school in the US. One astonishing young lady.

I spent most of the day in the room due to the rain. I got caught up on some reading and writing, and I even tried making coffee in the chorreador. I took a video of me brewing the coffee for shoots and giggles. That was an interesting experience! The coffee wasn't the best that I had ever tried, but it wasn't bad! I guess I just need more practice.

The next day was much drier. Swatty said that the rain was country-wide the day before and was very uncharacteristic. Before we could even give the rain a chance, we decided to do the tour early. Swatty walked me through their seven-acre organic farm, showing me the variety of fruits and veggies grown, along with their coffee plants. Unfortunately, coffee is harvested during our winter months, so all I could see were small green buds starting to grow. Anything that you eat or drink at the farm was grown on the farm. After the tour was over, I needed to go to the grocery store. Swatty mentioned that she and another friend were going into town and wanted to know if I wanted to go with them. They said that they would show me around town a bit and take me to a grocery store.

We started driving toward Santa Elena, and Swatty told me a little more about the town. It is a small town, mostly focused on tourism and coffee. I asked her about what locals do. She said that most locals work the majority of the week. The occasional time that they are off, they will go for a drink or go out into nature. I would imagine if I were surrounded by all of this nature, I would take every opportunity to take advantage of it as well. She mentioned that many people, including her family, like to go places and have picnics. Sounds wonderful to me!

She took me to a place at the top of the hill. We parked next to Morpho's Restaurant and walked across the street. Swatty wanted to show me the fallen fig tree. She said that it is something that many locals like to go and see and not all tourists know about it. I thought this tree was going to be in a town square or a park from the way she described it, but it wasn't. We had to hike down from the street toward a creek in the mud. Normally, this wouldn't be a big thing, but I had worn sandals and normal clothes to go to town. We both looked at my sandals and said, "Oops!" Pura vida!

We walked along the creek and as we crossed over the creek was the fig tree, which, more than likely due to all of the rain, had slid off a drop-off and fell over onto the other side, forming a bridge. Over time, the roots started to fall downwards from the tree at the trunk and created this exquisite formation. The roots are now into the creek and the ground and people can walk across the tree from one side to the other. I wish I could have done that, but my sandals weren't good enough to climb in the mud. The three of us talked throughout the small hike. Swatty's friend asked, "Do you drink (alcohol)?" "Claro!" I replied. When we got back to the car, Swatty and her friend wanted to take me to the local bar in town. Love it!

We arrived at Bar Amigos. Swatty left her backpack in the car and I asked, "Do you want to put your bag in the trunk where people can't see it?" She kind of gave me a funny look and replied, "No, it will be fine there. Why?" I mentioned that in La Fortuna, you can't leave belongings in cars, because there is so much theft, especially rental cars.

She said, "Oh, that rarely happens in Monteverde. There are cameras everywhere downtown. There was a break-in a couple of months ago by a Tico from another village. He was caught rather quickly." Already, I started to see the difference between Monteverde and La Fortuna.

Bar Amigos was just a typical bar and restaurant that had a wonderful view of the forest. The drinks were reasonable and they had small bar bites. One of their favorite bar bites was *salchipapas*, which were french fries with fried pieces of hot dog on top. Speaking my language! They even had their own kind of fry sauce, which looked like ketchup and mayo.

We had an enjoyable time at the bar. This was exactly what I was looking for in this trip: sitting with locals and feeling immersed in the culture and not into the tourism. Swatty told me that she had to help at her dad's hotel for the rest of my stay. I was bummed that I wouldn't see her again. One, she was such a sweet girl, but the other was that I was left to defend myself in Spanish at the farm, lol.

After food and drinks, Swatty took me to a local grocery store where I could find items cheaper than at the big supermarkets. She made sure to tell me not to get any produce at the store because I could have whatever I wanted on the farm. So awesome. I can't think of a time when I have had organic produce straight from a farm. Every moment that passed by, the more I fell in love with Monteverde.

When we got back to the farm, I mentioned to Hermida about grabbing some veggies from the greenhouse. She immediately took me to where they had their supply of ripe veggies and started to hand me as much as I could hold! I got a tomato, one veggie that I'm still trying to figure out what it was, and an avocado. This was the largest avocado that I have ever seen! It was a lovely shade of purple and perfectly ripe. I had to eat it in three separate sessions, it was so big! Everything tasted fresh and scrumptious.

I decided to cook in the room that night to try and save a little money. I had picked up a piece of pork meat at the grocery store and I was going to cook it on the stove. My family and friends were a little concerned about the stove, not because it was a gas stove, but because it was connected to a propane tank right next to it. I think they thought that I would blow up the casa. It did take me a few minutes to figure out how it worked. Hermida showed me how to turn the gas on and off. I flipped the propane switch like she showed me and turned the burner button like I normally would on a stove. I heard the gas going and I hit the ignite button on the side. Nothing happened ... hmmm. *What am I missing?* I thought to myself. I noticed on the counter that there was a set of matches. Oooh, maybe this was what my family was worried about lol. I was a little nervous myself at this point. I turned the gas down to the minimum. I slowly lit the match and held it over the burner. I hit the ignition button and prayed. It quickly lit and I got my hand out of the way as fast as I could. I should never doubt myself!

My dinner was delicious with the fresh pork and veggies. Everything tasted so fresh and I knew that I would miss this once I got back to the States. I decided to do the El Tigre Waterfall hike tomorrow, which starts early in the am. Got to crash early. Night!!

Day Four: I Think I Left My Undercarriage Back There - El Tigre Waterfalls

I had a little trouble sleeping last night due to extra bugs in the room, including a ginormous spider that kept eyeing me. I can handle bugs, but spiders freak me out.

I got up early, made some sock coffee, ate a peanut butter and banana sandwich, and then headed out the door to make it to El Tigre Waterfalls for a morning hike. I have mentioned in the past the condition of Monteverde roads: some of the worst roads that I have ever seen. They are unpaved and not even leveled out. They are very narrow and very steep. On the roads getting to El Tigre, I was so nervous that I was leaving the undercarriage of my small sedan in different places in Monteverde. Not even joking. I could hear the scraping and the occasional rock being thrown. I could see locals looking at me and I'm sure they were saying "dumb gringa" in Spanish and smirking.

It took me thirty minutes to get to El Tigre since I was going about five mph on average, but I made it. El Tigre is close to one of the high hilltops in Monteverde. The view was miraculous the moment you got out of the car.

At the reception desk, I had my temperature taken, got a bracelet on my wrist, and had the trail explained to me. They also offered a free bamboo stick to walk with. That bamboo stick saved me. It even made me start to think that I may need some sort of stick for future hikes.

They tell you that there are four waterfalls, but in reality, there are many more. There are "mini-waterfalls" throughout the trail. And what a stunning trail. In the first half, I descended into the forest. There were a couple of steep steps and I had to trek through a creek a few times while navigating rocks. Luckily, that was when the bamboo stick came in handy. Immersed in the rainforest, I was surrounded by greenery, but it was very open and I went in and out of shade and sunshine. Especially with the increased altitude, I could really feel and breathe in the fresh air. I didn't see many animals around. The only sounds that I heard were the rushing of water from all of the waterfalls and rivers, along with the faint chirping of the surrounding birds in the trees.

The trail was not crowded at all and I rarely ran into people. By the time I reached a waterfall to take pictures, a few people were just leaving and more people arrived.

The path was well-maintained but rocky, and the signage was clear. No wrong turns this time for this girl! There were several suspension bridges that freaked me out a little. Most had signs that six or fewer people could be on them at a time. There were a few that were just a long piece of board and said only one at a time. There were handrails here and there throughout the trail, which is good if someone went without a stick.

The last waterfall was somewhat of a hike, no pun intended. It was about 300 meters, but all uphill and mostly steps. It was worth it though. I had even asked the reception guy if it was worth the trouble—he assured me it was. I 100 percent agree. It was a gorgeous waterfall where I could get a little closer than the others. There were smaller waterfalls that were cascading through lush green vines. The walls surrounding the waterfall were where Instagram cafes get their décor ideas from. There were also rocks and level places where I could sit and rest, take pictures, or swim.

Along the way, there were boxes that had walkie-talkies in them, so you could call for help if needed. For someone who has been alone on many hikes, I wish that this was more popular on other trails and parks. They said that once you reach box three, you need to call them and tell them that you are there. Once they get your call, they start to get your horse ready for when you reach point four. It was a steep hike up to point four, but there was a breathtaking walk along a creek with a cool breeze that cooled me off from the hike. I could tell when I was getting closer: the faint smell of horse poop grows as you walk along the trail.

It took me about two hours to get through the trail. My watch said that I walked about two and a half miles. Not too bad, I guess. I was definitely ready to rest and enjoy my horse ride. Even though the trail is self-guided, they luckily have a guide that rides with you while you are on the horse. The road back up to the reception house was rocky and steep. I am glad that I was on a horse and not walking this. My horse's name was Canelo, a sweet horse that really liked to ride next to the other horse that someone was riding on. My leg tended to rub against both of the sides of the two horses. Luckily, it wasn't hard enough to get caught or cause injury.

By the time we got off the horses, I was thirsty and ready to eat. We walked past the reception desk into the kitchen and dining area. It was an open room where the cooks are cooking on a very large flat-top stove that is supported by bricks and heated by firewood below with a chimney coming up through the ceiling. I loved seeing the traditional way of cooking and the smell was indescribable! Even though I was so hot and sweaty, I rarely turned down a cup of coffee. The coffee along with blueberry juice was delicious.

The lunch and coffee were included in the tour price, which was perfect. I preordered the arroz con pollo dish, which was ready within a few minutes. They had a long wooden bar along the patio of the house, where you can sit to eat and look out at the magnificent panoramic view of the awe-inspiring Monteverde mountains. The whole morning was completely spectacular and worth the awful drive. Of course, that also reminded me that I now had to make that drive back down. Argh.

I had to drive slowly, but the drive wasn't as bad as it was coming up, probably because I knew what to expect. Right when I got back to the farm, it started to pour down rain. Good timing! I could tell that I was blessed that day. Going to get some rest and start getting my things together. Have to leave the farm in the morning and head to a new destination within Monteverde. Yay!

Day Five: Coffee Cupping & A Night Walk

I woke up this morning, made some breakfast and sock coffee, and then started getting all my belongings packed up into the car to leave the farm. It was a great experience, and I wished I could have stayed longer to possibly try cooking lessons with Hermida or explore the farm more. I'm leaving today to go across Santa Elena to a bungalow at Sunset Hills.

I tried to say goodbye to Hermida and pay my tab, but she was away from the house. I left the money for the tab, wrote in their guest book, and headed out. I had a few hours to kill before my check-in time, so I decided to explore Santa Elena a little more. When I rode through town with Swatty a few days ago, I saw several cute shops, along with coffee shops. Santa Elena is a region that is well-known for its coffee.

I did some window shopping in some of the souvenir shops downtown. I window-shopped so much that I became hungry and also thirsty for coffee. I went into Cafe de Monteverde and got a cold brew coffee, along with one of the best banana breads that I have ever eaten. It could have been because I was hungry, but it was so delicious. It was very moist and had a layer of chocolate on top ... mmmmm ... chocolate. As I was sitting there with my coffee and banana bread, I was looking around the cafe. I had contemplated doing another coffee tour before checking into my room, but I had learned quite a bit from the La Fortuna tour and other tours that I have done in the past. I spoke with the barista and she mentioned that you can drive to Cafe de Monteverde plantation anytime and walk around on your own. Well, there's an idea!

I drove over to the plantation and spoke with Daniel. I had asked him if his company ever did cuppings. He said that they had done some in the past, but not since Covid. He asked if I would like to have one. If that isn't a silly question; of course, I would! We negotiated a price of fifteen dollars to do a five roast coffee cupping and I could drink as much as I want. Score! Just in case you haven't heard of coffee cupping, it is basically wine-tasting, but with coffee. There is a lot more involved, but let's just keep it simple.

As they were making the coffee, I walked around their plantation and looked to see what varieties they had planted. They have quite a few varieties, including Geisha, which many coffee producers try to grow now. Since it was June, coffee cherries were not quite halfway through their growing process. They looked like little green limes starting to grow.

After walking around and taking a few pics, I went inside. Right when I walked in, there was an aroma of heavenly bliss ... coffee brewing. Daniel had ground up five different types of beans and was brewing them in French presses. It was almost ready when I first walked up to the table. The coffee was sitting very high on the press and looked almost like chocolate souffle or cake. He said that the beans had just been roasted about twenty-four to forty-eight hours before. I couldn't remember the last time that I had coffee that has been roasted that soon. He explained that there was still a good bit of CO_2 in the coffee, which makes the grounds expand upon brewing.

At their plantation, they did all three processes: washed, natural, and honey. We got to try all three. For washed, he brewed light, medium, and dark roast. Daniel said that they typically roast natural and honey processed beans to medium, so we got to try those as well. Every one of them was excellent, even the dark roast, which I'm not usually a fan of. My favorite was the natural process and surprisingly my least favorite was the honey. I would have thought that the honey process coffee would have been slightly sweeter and that I would have been able to taste more defined notes than I did. Either way, I drank my fifteen dollars worth of each one! I even took some natural home with me.

After my coffee cupping, it was time to check in to the new Airbnb. I got the key and then drove just a bit outside of town onto a gravel road. Yes, I know, another gravel road in Monteverde. I passed a large gate and eventually onto my own personal driveway. I walked along a long concrete bridge to the front door under a small forest of trees. It looked a little dark. I opened the front door, and suddenly all this light came shining through. The whole back side of the room had floor-to-ceiling windows that exposed breathtaking views of the Monteverde Cloud Forest and the entire mountainside. I could even see Lake Arenal all the way in the back. I just stood there in the middle of the room, taking in all the majestic beauty in awe, and couldn't believe that this room actually existed.

As I looked around, it was like a modern mountain cabin. There was a tree that came up through the floor and ceiling right in the middle of the cabin. There were two large boulders, not rocks, but boulders sitting in the room. It almost looked like they built the room/cabin around them. From the wall of windows, there was a balcony with two wooden chairs. Inside from the balcony was almost like a little nook, where you were surrounded by glass with two swinging wicker egg chairs. I don't care where I buy another home, but it will definitely have swinging wicker egg chairs after this visit to Costa Rica.

The shower was a large walk-in that was just a large piece of wood, a rainfall shower head, and one long piece of glass off to the side. As you took a shower and turned away from the wall, you faced another extremely large window looking out at the same view as the rest of the room. I wish I could have stayed here longer. On top of that, the shower was scalding hot, just the way I like it! After all the cold showers on the finca, I welcomed the warmth with open arms.

After unpacking and resting, I scheduled to be a part of the Kinkajou Night Walk. I had heard from several people and had read a few blog posts that a night walk was a great way to see some fauna. It was only twenty-five dollars, so I figured it was worth a try.

It was drizzling when I got to the Night Walk. I was concerned because it was raining pretty hard right before I left the room. I was in a group of five and it was the first tour where they still made you wear your mask. I paid for the tour when I arrived. Even though they had a card machine, the man taking payment refused to take my credit card. He only wanted cash. Unfortunately, he took what cash I had left and so I didn't have any left to tip the tour guide. Bummer for that, because our guide was very good.

Our tour guide, Donald, was funny and passionate about nature and wildlife. He really did try to help us find wildlife. He even took pictures with our cameras that turned out looking like professional pictures. As he would jokingly say, "I'm a professional." Haha. We did see quite a few fauna out there. Not as much as I would hope, but overall, it was still a good experience. We saw an orange-kneed tarantula, a toucan, two kinds of motmot birds, and a scorpion that Donald made glow in blacklight. We saw multiple frogs, most I don't know the names of. One frog had red eyes and can only be found in Costa Rica, but it wasn't the red-eyed tree frog that is so famous. We saw glass frog eggs on a leaf. It was a cool video to see the tadpoles swim within the egg. We also caught a glimpse of two frogs mating. During my last visit to Costa Rica, I saw two turtles mating in the ocean from my boat. Must be the thing to do around here!

I really, really wanted to see a sloth. We looked and looked. Finally, Donald got a call on his walkie-talkie that they saw one. We did see it, but it was waaaay up in a tree and we could only see the back of the sloth. It just looked like a brown blob attached to a tree. I'll have to keep looking for more sloths along my journey.

All in all, I thought it was a good tour and it included transportation. I was ready to eat and crash when I got back to the room. Tomorrow will be an exciting day. If the weather still holds up, I'm going to hike through Monteverde Cloud Forest Reserve, and at 5 pm will be my reservation for the San Lucas Treetop dining experience! Excited!!

Day Six: Monteverde Cloud Forest Reserve & My Treetop Dining Experience

Without A/C, this room at Sunset Hills was just cool enough so that I slept really well. I did wake up here and there because I had another extremely large arachnoid friend staring at me across the room. I always have this fear of waking up with a spider on my face. Don't tell me I'm alone in this, am I???

The room had an American-style coffeemaker that made twelve cups. This place is starting to top my faves list! I made a pot of coffee and sat in my swing chair and just enjoyed the silence and peacefulness. Unfortunately, there was a good bit of fog and clouds covering the view, but it didn't bother me much. I felt so relaxed and at peace that it could have been raining and I still would have been just as content. I took another scalding shower and it took everything I had to get out of it. When you go almost three weeks without a hot shower, trust me, you won't take it for granted again.

I made my way up to Monteverde Cloud Forest Reserve. Parking along the road was free, but it was another narrow road that was already starting to get packed upon arrival around 10 am. They have a paid parking lot for five dollars and it was 0.6 miles away from the entrance.

They had a free shuttle that would take hikers back and forth. One warning, they will sit there in the lot until they decide that they are ready to drive up and down. They also don't seem too happy with what they're doing.

Approaching the entrance, everything was pretty well organized. They had a place to wash hands, take your temp, and then pay for the ticket and parking. Walking out, there was another person standing by a large trail (*sendero*) map to assist hikers in figuring out the best trail plan. I told him that I wanted to walk for about three hours. He told me to start on the trail to the waterfall, which is very short and close by. From there, I would get on the Sendero Tosi. It would then bypass Sendero Wilford Guindon, taking me to the suspension bridge. When I was there, the bridge was closed due to it being broken. When you look at it, you can totally tell why. Yikes! From there, get on the Sendero Camino to the Sendero La Ventana. This would take me to the farthest point at the Continental Divide. From there, I would get onto Sendero Nuboso, which takes you back to the beginning. This was roughly 4.35 miles, and he said it should take me about three hours. You got all that, right?

I started up the Waterfall trail. There was a somewhat steep incline to the trail, but not as bad as some that I have already hiked. The trail was maintained and was somewhat flat and leveled out. No navigating over moving rocks or gravel to trip me up. It was a short walk to the waterfall. And there was no swimming allowed. The waterfall was pretty, but it was smaller than most that I have seen. It was still worth the small hike.

I started to venture down and I found the sign for Sendero Tosi. Most of the trails are very clearly marked and have good signage. The only time that I got a little confused was once I got to the Sendero Chomogo and Wilford Guindon. Getting to the break in the trail, there was a sign for Sendero Chomogo, but not Wilford Guindon. I had to hike a bit on Chomogo and it took me to another break where Wilford Guindon began. It took me a minute to figure that out, along with a little bit of backtracking.

Once I got on Sendero Wilford Guindon, the trail changed a bit. It wasn't quite as level and there were a bit more broken steps. It also became steeper but at a decline. I did slip a couple of times due to the mud, but nothing major. The majority of the time that I was hiking, I was alone. It was good in a way because it was quiet and I was hoping to see more fauna. I heard a couple of birds in the distance, but I never really saw anything. Even the noises that I heard within the forest were not as loud as I have been used to hearing in other parts of the rainforest.

I kept stopping every few moments to rest for a moment and look up into the trees and out into the forest. Nothing. I barely saw any movements within the branches and leaves and that was only because of the wind. Along with no movements, there was barely any noise. At times, it was almost eerily silent, until I would hear a human walk by on a different trail.

I passed the suspension bridge, which looked like someone had taken both sides and twisted it like wringing out clothes. No bueno. I would hate to be the people on the bridge when it broke like that. I then continued on the trail to the Continental Divide. I got on Sendero Camino and this trail was probably the worst out of all of them. It is wide, but they must have had an issue with flooding or maintaining the trail. It was very muddy, sometimes to the point where I would slide in the mud. There wasn't even close to the same amount of gravel/rock or cement levelers as the other trails.

I reached La Ventana. There was a platform at the top as a lookout. There were two girls sitting out on the platform eating lunch. It was actually a pretty good idea: I wish I would have thought of that. There was a decent view and also a cool breeze at the top to sit and rest. There were signs that the wind can get pretty strong at the top. Monteverde is very well known for its wind. It was breezy that day, but nothing crazy.

Clouds and fog can also be a problem up there. On the other side, by the "Smooth Forest," there was too much fog for me to really see anything. At La Ventana, I could see almost everything. It was pretty clear. If it wasn't for the sign stating that it was the Continental Divide, I wouldn't have known. The point of the Divide is where the water goes in different directions to the Pacific and Atlantic Oceans. Unfortunately, because of the forest and potentially the altitude, you can't see any water or anything that shows a change. A great lookout either way though.

I finished up the hike by walking along Sendero Nuboso. There were a few more signs telling more about the forest. A few of the signs did mention that there are fewer and fewer fauna over the years due to lack of food. Even though it was a nice hike and a pretty forest, if you are wanting to see more than trees, this may not be the hike for you. I definitely don't think it is worth thirty dollars anymore. It is one of the priciest parks that I have encountered so far. To really see fauna there, I believe that you can hire a guide who is able to point out fauna using their equipment, but that also comes at a hefty price.

After the Cloud Forest, I was hungry and had a need for coffee. After looking through Tripadvisor for reviews, I noticed that Choco Cafe was along the way and seemed to be a frequent tourist spot for those leaving the forest. I stopped in and had one of the best moccachinos that I have ever had. I also ordered a tricolor fusilli with smoked salmon, which sounded yummy and different. It totally was. It was just enough and I wasn't overly full from the pasta. The flavors complemented each other well and the cream sauce didn't overpower the salmon. Great lunch for fourteen dollars after tax and tip. I checked out a couple more shops around the area and then decided to go and rest up before my dinner.

San Lucas Treetop experience is in Chira Glamping, which is a unique hotel in itself. I wish I could have tried it before I left Monteverde; maybe next time. I arrived for my reservation a few minutes early and was escorted down to the restaurant and greeted by the waiter. He explained how the whole experience works, and he walked me to my own glass house. Mine had a small table and one chair just for me. There was a small cooler and a coat rack inside the room. It was completely glass, except for the floor. It even shook slightly when people walked down the walkway. There was a panoramic view of Santa Elena, Monteverde, and a few other small villages. Unfortunately, my house had a slightly obscured view due to trees, but nothing that would make me not enjoy the experience or the view.

There were only five tables/houses with lantern lights everywhere. The 5 pm seating was the perfect time to watch the sunset while eating. That was actually the first sunset that I was able to see since I arrived in Costa Rica three weeks ago. It was still somewhat cloudy, but hardly any rain.

The experience was a seven-course prix fixe menu. There are no substitutions, but they will accommodate based on allergies or beliefs. I chose the normal menu, which served meat and seafood. I also chose the wine pairing. The total with tax and tip was $146. It was definitely one of the most expensive meals that I have ever had for myself. The second most expensive was at Cafe Des Artistes in Puerto Vallarta, Mexico, and that was only $120.

The first course was veggies in a flowerpot. They used truffles and olives to create "dirt." As part of the experience, they poured water into the flower bed and the veggies rose as if they were growing. Pretty cool concept. That was then followed by chicken pate and hummus with bread, then sashimi fish with pork rinds on top and slightly citrusy ponzu sauce. The sashimi wasn't as tender as I would have hoped and had to be cut with a knife. It was still very light and tasty.

After the sashimi was the fourth course, grilled octopus with cheese fondue. The grilled octopus was in small pieces with more pork rinds. The waiter created a cheese fondue in a pot in front of me and said that it was a traditional fondue with cheese from the Quakers who settled there. There was a lot of cheese on my plate. It was very creamy with great flavor, but I didn't think that it complemented the octopus very well.

Next was the main course, lamb. They didn't ask me about the temperature of the meat beforehand, so I asked the waiter. He said that they normally cook the meat about medium well and maybe a little more. Medium well lamb? Not really what I was looking for. He asked if that was ok, and I said to please not cook it any more than medium. The lamb came out in small tenderloin pieces. I guess that is why there is a temperature problem. It was cooked closer to medium well. Unfortunately, it was not my favorite dish.

As I was finishing the lamb, there was smoke or a slight fog that started to enter the room. I realized quickly that it was part of the experience. The waiter walked in with a well-presented plate for dessert. It was a type of sorbet, cookie, and what seemed like a type of flan. It was served under a white dome on a wooden plate with succulents. Very pretty.

Soon after, the waiter brought over a locked box that was placed in the room after the first course. After taking off the lock, he opened up the box to reveal another dessert that looked like a jail cell. Another part of the box was a printed picture that they had taken of me when I first arrived. It was very creative and well thought out.

I wasn't overly impressed with the wine that was paired with the food or the amount that was given for the price. When it was all said and done, I believe that I was paying more for ambiance and experience than the actual food itself, which is ok. I did walk away a little hungry and sober. Would I recommend it to others? If you want an interesting experience in Monteverde, yes. I would recommend it more for couples due to the romantic atmosphere that is created.

Once I got back to my cabin, another spider friend was back and bigger than the rest. It was on the wall above one of the boulders. I kept trying to sweep it off the wall to try and get it out of the cabin, but it wasn't working. My bf had mentioned killing it with a shoe, but it was almost as big as my shoe and I didn't want my hand that close to it. So what does Kelly do? She reaches for a frying pan from the kitchen. I then had to climb on the boulder to try and get to the spider. Of course, I missed the spider, fell off the boulder, and ran screaming like a pansy across the cabin. It was something that you would see in a silly comedy movie and not something that would be believable in real life. Overall, not bad for my last night in Monteverde. In the morning, I will be headed back to La Fortuna. Not looking forward to that drive. Fingers crossed that it goes well!! :D

Day Seven: Sad To Leave, But Fortuna Bound

No spiders or bugs visited me during the night, so that was a major plus and a great way to start the morning. There were hardly any clouds when I woke up and you could see all the way to Lake Arenal from my balcony. It was a postcard view! I made some coffee and took in the view while journaling and watching the stock market. If every Monday could be like this, we would never have bad Mondays.

After coffee, I showered and packed up all my belongings once again. It was time to head back to La Fortuna. I wish I could have stayed in Monteverde a little longer. I came to enjoy Monteverde a little more than La Fortuna. People seemed to be a little nicer and just the overall feel of Monteverde just seemed nicer. Monteverde almost made La Fortuna feel a little ghetto. I'm not saying that La Fortuna is ghetto, for those that may be offended, but between the two cities, I preferred Monteverde. Take it or leave it.

Before getting on the road, I stopped at the market to get a few veggies and wine, because the prices seem a bit cheaper here. I also stopped at Choco Cafe one more time for a moccachino (how could I not?) and a brownie for the ride.

My Last Days at the Volcano

Days 1-9: My Last Days at the Volcano

The ride was a little better leaving Monteverde since I didn't have to go near Viento Fresco. The roads were more paved and level. I didn't hit much traffic until I got to Aguacate, which is about the halfway point. The second half was a bit slower due to getting behind a few slow cars and trucks, but I made it in two and a half hours, which is pretty good.

After unpacking into my loft from before, I knew I was hungry. I stopped back by Soda Viquez. Diego didn't recognize me, which is understandable; he sees so many people on a daily basis. After a few moments, he said that he remembered me and thanked me for coming back again. He asked how I liked Monteverde and I thanked him for all the great suggestions that he gave before on hidden gems to visit. We spoke for a few more minutes and then his shift was over. I got my usual casado con pescado, which is always fresh and hits the hunger spot perfectly.

When I got up to pay my check, Diego's mother and owner cashed me out. She thanked me for coming back to see them again. She then gave me a large sticker that said, "I Love Costa Rica." How sweet! This is definitely one of my favorite places here in La Fortuna and I will always encourage people to visit.

The next day, I signed up for a kayaking tour of Lake Arenal. There was no hotel pickup, but the office was close to Red Frog Roasters. I was a little hungry and craving a pastry. I saw a bakery along one of the main roads and went for a quick bite. I stopped at Panaderia La Principal and it took me a few minutes to decide because they had so much variety. I bought one of their custard donuts with chocolate on top. To die for! I would probably have to stop by here at least once more before leaving Fortuna.

Once I arrived at the office, we had to sit around for a bit before they took our temperatures, then they piled us into their van. The ride to the dock where our kayaks were was about a forty-five minute drive. It was in a small village where you could see locals and their families on the lake shore with tents and tables for their family fun time picnic.

They only had two-person kayaks and I was the only single person on the tour. The guide got in the kayak with me and we started to kayak through the lake. It was a beautiful day out and I was blessed again with the weather. The sun was out with few clouds and I could see the volcano rather clearly. Kayaking on the lake is where you are able to get the closest to the volcano to see all of its majestic beauty. The guide had us kayak to a secluded area of the lake where cars couldn't get to. He made a fruit spread for us on the shore and some people swam in the lake. In the distance, we could hear howler monkeys starting to howl. The guide informed us that meant that we were getting rain soon. Sure enough, in about five to ten minutes it started raining. Just a light sprinkle, but the howlers like to announce when rain is here or when it is coming.

As we kayaked back to the starting point, we saw bicycles in the lake. Yup, read that again. Bicycles in the lake. From afar, I could only see the bikes and was confused. I then saw that the bikes were on two banana-boat-like rafts and people still pedaled like they would on the ground. It looked like so much fun! This would be on my to-do list if I get to come back or see it somewhere else.

My last few days spent in La Fortuna were mostly doing work inside, while only going to get coffee and meals. It rained pretty hard several days in a row and I just took the time to rest. I got to try more great dishes at some of my favorite restaurants in town. I think that the rain was starting to get to me and I was beginning to feel a little gloomy. When it rains in La Fortuna, you are pretty limited on what activities you can do. I think there was another part of me that was just ready for the beach, my happy place!

I spent a little over three weeks in La Fortuna. One thing to notice about any place in Costa Rica, they do not leave their A/C on if they are not home. Electricity is very expensive in Costa Rica. I'm starting to think that everything is expensive in Costa Rica and it might be the most expensive country in Latin America.

For the most part, everyone was very nice in La Fortuna. In most restaurants that I went to, the customer service was great. I had many servers make recommendations of places to go, including places that locals like to go. These were mostly men. I did notice that men would typically start a conversation more than women. Most women in restaurants and grocery stores had mundane facial expressions and barely spoke.

The women in the Kolbi ICE office... don't even get me started! I did, however, meet a nice woman in a cute clothing store who was very hospitable and we were joking around together, especially when none of the clothes would fit me. My guide at Don Juan Coffee Tours was also very nice and talkative. That was a nice change. Overall, it feels that male workers are out having fun and the women are all business when they converse with you. To each their own.

Some of my favorite places were Red Frog Roasters, Soda Viquez, Snapper's, and Restaurante Cafe Mediterraneo. The worst was Soda La Hormiga. They had the worst customer service every time I went in. The food was mediocre at best but I continued to go back because it was also the cheapest that I could find in town while trying to keep to a budget. It was totally worth the extra fifty cents to a dollar more to go around the corner (literally) and go to Soda Viquez. Much better quality, value, and the people are just great over there.

Being there during Covid, there seemed to be some restaurant casualties. Now, some places could have been closed up because it was rainy season and they felt it was better to close with decreased tourists, but most seemed due to not being able to handle the fifty percent capacity, a similar story that I heard so often in the States.

There was no way to know if a restaurant was going to be open or not. I frequented Red Frog Roasters multiple days a week for my iced coffee fix. On my last day in La Fortuna, a Wednesday, I drove by to get coffee on my way out of town and they were closed up. A week or so before I left town, they started closing on Wednesdays, which is common in CR. Not all of the sites that list their business had updated the hours yet.

Tripadvisor and Google Maps are not reliable here regarding whether a place is open or not. Chipotle said temporarily closed, but it was open when I walked by. Taconga Tacos said it was open on Tripadvisor, Google Maps, along with Facebook too. I walked by, and everything was locked up. Walked by a few more times after that and the whole shopping plaza was locked up and didn't open once, even though their website said they were open. It is definitely a gamble when you are a tourist and you set out to grab dinner.

Other Things to do in La Fortuna

Obviously, I didn't get to do all of the activities that are offered in La Fortuna. Some activities I did on my first visit to this country, and I wanted to try new things.

Here are more ideas of what you can do here:

1. Bogarin Trail- A touristy area where there are supposedly sloths everywhere. It was too expensive for me and felt like a zoo for the poor sloths. I might totally be wrong.

2. Ziplining is very big here and La Fortuna was the first place that I have ever gotten to do it.

3. Mistico Arenal Hanging Bridges - I did this on my first trip and if you are cool with heights and suspension bridges, it is worth checking out.

4. Waterfall canyoneering

5. Whitewater rafting

6. El Silencio Trail - I didn't get to try this one, because they only take cash. I drove out there and at that time, their website didn't mention cash only and they only take colones. The attendant was not very nice about

it, so I didn't feel that it was worth driving all the way back. It has good ratings online, but there are many places to hike around the area.

7. Cooking classes

8. ATV tours around the volcano

I'm sure there are many more. There are endless options in this area.

Playas Del Coco

Days 1-3: Learning the Lay of the Land

Playas Del Coco was one of the highlights of my trip. This city had almost everything I was looking for. A quiet and beautiful beach, not too touristy, with locals everywhere, everything within close proximity, good food, and easy to travel to other locations. I had booked an Airbnb condo a mile or so off of the main strip but within walking distance of the beach. I booked it for a month, which was so much cheaper than a week or two. For the most part, my condo had everything that I needed. The A/C worked great and it had a large, well-stocked kitchen. There were a few things that went south during my stay, but the hosts were very responsive with fixing things. On the first day, the coffeemaker was completely broken, but they brought me another one that day. They had to replace the hot water heater and washing machine, along with having to fix a leaking vanity in the bathroom. It was so nice having a washing machine again and not having to wash my clothes in the sink.

The beach itself has grey to black colored sand. I read some people's comments that the sand looks dirty, but I thought it was gorgeous. On top of the grayish-black color, it had a wonderful sparkle as you walked along. It almost looked like a small girl threw glitter around, but in a delightful way. During low tide, the beach was spacious and the sand was very soft. There were very few pebbles or shells that I encountered. Now, during high tide, most of the beach was lost, but that is common among many beaches within Costa Rica.

The water was not super clear, but it had a light royal blue and emerald green coloring throughout the cove of this beach. Toward the north end of the beach, there was a smaller cove that had clearer, emerald-green water. The water was very calm. It is definitely not a place for surfers, but more for those who want to chill and relax.

The beach is also very quiet. I was there during the month of July, which is still considered the rainy or "off" season. During the week, I would be one of maybe two to five people at a time on this beach. This was toward the end of the north side of the beach where my Airbnb was located. Toward the main strip, there were more people, but still fewer than some of the other beaches that I visited during the week. On the weekends, the beach becomes much livelier. It was a great experience for me because you didn't see tons of Americans or other foreigners as you do at Jaco or Tamarindo, but more locals and their families.

I met a local on the beach. His name was Andres and worked for a local tour company. As I was lying there, he approached me and asked if he could sit next to me. I replied, "Sure," even though the beach was basically empty. We exchanged pleasantries as I struggled with my Spanglish.

"What do the locals do when they are not working?" I asked.

"Most of the time, we enjoy coming out onto the beach, bringing tables and chairs, and having bonfires with drinks. We can't really afford the drink prices at most of the restaurants and bars on the main strip, so it is cheaper for us to come out here. It is also a good place to go since everything closes at 9 pm because of Covid," he replied.

It sounded similar to what we enjoyed back in the southern country-side where I am from, but by a wheat field instead of the beach. After some time, he kept wanting to talk and I just wanted to relax in the sun. Do you ever find yourself in a situation where you are done talking with someone, but you don't know how to end the conversation without feeling rude? I eventually just had to get up and leave, because he didn't want to stop talking.

As I was leaving, he asked, "Come back tonight for a bonfire?"

"I have a Facetime date with my boyfriend tonight, but thank you," I replied.

"Ok, no problem. Give me your number and we will do a different night," he said with persistence.

I politely declined. During my stay I saw him a few other times go up to more women on the beach and strike up conversations. We would wave to each other from a distance as he would go back to his conversation.

Along the main strip, there are many restaurants, souvenir shops, pharmacies, and grocery stores. A basketball court and soccer field right along the beach were packed full of people playing on the weekends.

Restaurants are typically closed on Wednesdays and some on Mondays. Coco has a variety of restaurants that could fit anyone's budget. Since it is smaller than La Fortuna, I noticed that the selection was smaller. I guess being on the beach, the prices were slightly higher than Fortuna as well, but not by much. A traditional casado that I could find for five dollars in Fortuna was on average around seven to eight dollars in Coco. Of course, being so close to the beach, Coco had some great seafood restaurants and the prices were reasonable. You can easily get a full seafood meal for fifteen dollars on average. One of my favorites, which is somewhat of a hidden gem, was Restaurante Mar Azul.

There is also a great selection of grocery stores. In Fortuna, I noticed that they pretty much just had the basics. There are some basic grocery stores in Coco, but they also have "supermarkets" as well. Auto Supermercado was one of my favorite stores in Coco. Luperon was also another one of my favorites. I would often times go to both to do price checks on certain items. Some things would be cheaper at one than the other. Auto Supermercado, on the other hand, had more upscale items and also more Americanized items. I found this great smelling body wash that was so cheap and it was from Palmolive. I had no idea that Palmolive made body wash. I do wish that they sold it in the States!

To try and keep my budget low, I would buy things at the grocery store to cook at home. They had a nice selection of pre-cooked foods, like tuna salad, macaroni salad, etc. Occasionally, I would get some macaroni salad, but my favorite was arroz con carne (rice with beef), which is more like fried rice with veggies with pieces of meat throughout. It was very tasty. I could get a small container for about four dollars and eat it with whatever meat I decided to cook that night for a pretty tasty and balanced meal.

Of course, it wouldn't be Costa Rica without several coffee shops. My favorite was Guayoyo Coffee House. It was technically an American-style coffee shop. The owner was from Georgia in the US and everyone there speaks English. I still tried to speak Spanish out of respect, but the majority of the time they would answer in English. They had the traditional espressos and lattes that most Americans drink, but also offered cold brew and their own chorreador like most Costa Rican shops. I don't think there was anything there that I didn't like. I even enjoyed their double protein cappuccino. I'm sure it wasn't healthy, but it made me feel like I was drinking healthy, lol. If you decide to visit this place, please do not leave without trying one of their homemade red velvet cookies. Ooommmggg. Insert drool emoji here.

Water shortage tended to happen more in Coco than I experienced in other cities. There was no warning and no real way to figure out how long the shortage would last. I learned my lesson by always taking a shower first thing in the morning if there was water, just in case.

Like most of Costa Rica, the locals were very welcoming. No place is perfect though and I did run into a couple of people who were not as friendly, but it was very few and far between. I had one woman follow me through a souvenir store. I guess she thought I was going to steal something, I don't know. All I do know is that it was very uncomfortable because she didn't just follow from a distance. She was very close by. Every time I would look up or turn around, she would be there. It was the one time when I really wanted to use the six-foot social distance rule.

Day Four: OMG, Do I Finally Get to See a Sloth?!?!

Throughout my stay in Costa Rica, I struggled to see sloths. I struggled to see most fauna due to staying during the rainy season and I also didn't want to spend a lot on tours and guides. During the rainy season, most animals stay deep within the forest, because it is easy for them to get water. Sloths tend to hang out high up in trees and do not come down but once a week.

I had heard reviews of Diamante and did some research. Diamante had many activities that you could purchase. I only wanted to see the animal sanctuary and meet Lucy, their sloth. It was forty-two dollars after tax since I was able to find a promo code online for 10 percent off. It was still pricey, but I was hoping it was worth it.

It's not a far drive from Playas Del Coco and there were quite a few signs telling what direction to go. Upon arrival, there was quite a large sign with the name off to the right and a dirt road to turn onto. The road was uneven with potholes and was steep, like many roads in Costa Rica. On my way out of the park, my undercarriage scraped along the road because of how uneven the road was. As I looked around and saw how much money they were making, there is absolutely no reason why their driveway couldn't at least be leveled out, if not paved like the rest of the park.

I arrived at the reception desk, and they gave me a bracelet and told me the transportation would be there in fifteen minutes. I walked around for a bit to look in the gift shop. I asked about coffee, but they said their small iced coffee was six dollars ... ouch!

As I waited, I saw multiple trolleys come up, dropping people off. The one thing that I noticed is that there wasn't anything written on any of them. There was no way to tell which trolley went to what part of the park. I finally walked back up to the reception desk and asked. They pointed to one trolley that had been sitting there for a few minutes. I got in and it was a short drive to the animal sanctuary.

For the most part, it felt like a zoo. A zoo wasn't really what I wanted. Most people that are here want to see the animals in their own habitat, which can be difficult to see at times. The one thing that I did like about this sanctuary was that it took injured animals or ones that cannot be in the wild on their own and took care of them. I at least told myself that it was good that they were here and that they were taking care of them. I saw frogs, butterflies, parrots, and toucans. For jungle cats, they had a puma, ocelot, jaguar, and margay. They were all in separate homes. I also saw multiple types of monkeys.

Then there they were, sloths. What I really liked about the sloths was that they were not in an enclosed home. They had a large tree in the middle of the sanctuary where the sloths stayed. I also liked that the tree wasn't that high, so you could even be at eye level with a sloth. For the most part, sloths are usually sleeping most of the time and don't move much. While I was there, I felt like one of the sloths knew that I was really there to see her and she put on a little show for me. She scratched herself a bit while hanging off of a branch. Then, she climbed down a branch slowly and laid on her back while still hanging on the branch above. As I was taking pictures of her, I even felt like she was posing for me. So cute! It made me so happy!

I walked around a little further through the reptile area and that was the end. I waited for a few minutes for the ride back to the reception area. The trolley parked, but the driver didn't say anything to us. As we got off, we saw other people getting back onto the trolley. I went to the reception and asked when the trolley to get to the parking lot would be there. She pointed to the one that I just got off of. Seriously?! There is a big lack of communication within the park. I could have just stayed on the trolley. By the time I walked back over, the trolley was already full and the other people who had gotten off with me, along with myself, had to stand and wait for another trolley. Argh.

The park really wasn't as big as I thought it would be, especially for the price. If you are struggling to see certain animals and are short on cash and time, this might be the place to visit. If you have more time or patience, you could probably skip this place.

Day Five: Catfished Airbnb Experience - La Leona Waterfall

La Leona Waterfall was recommended in multiple blog posts. It is a pretty dangerous hike without a guide and a guide is now mandatory to visit the farm. It is located on a private estate called Finca Don Rafa. It was also recommended on the official website to use a local guide. It gave two links to tour guides. I chose Airbnb. I chose wrong.

Unfortunately, for any other history or facts about the property, I would just have to regurgitate from other blog posts. I'll explain why.

I got a message from the tour owner, Jonathan, the day before the hike. I had decided to go on the hike on a certain day because I already had my rental car switch scheduled in Liberia. Two birds, one stone, blah, blah, blah. He asked if he could change the time to an hour later than scheduled. He said that it had been raining a lot at night and wanted to make sure the river wasn't too brown from the rain. I agreed. He tried to change it to be even later, but I said that I was on a time crunch due to having to be at the rental car place. He said no problem and to be there at 10 am.

I arrived at the Soda, which was our meeting point. Jonathan approached my car and introduced himself. He said that I should leave almost everything in my car, except bug spray, sunscreen, and phone. He gave me a dry bag to use during the hike. After I placed everything in the bag and was ready to go, he said that he only goes on the tours every other day and Fernanda would be my guide today. He pointed to a truck for me to get into in order to get into the entrance of the farm. At the end of the drive, neither the driver nor Fernanda said anything. She just started walking toward the trail entrance and then waved her hand at me to come. Hmmm, this should be interesting.

The trail is steep and narrow. There are guiding ropes throughout, which are definitely needed to help stabilize. The trail was slightly muddy, but not awful. I didn't slip one time, and I was wearing my water shoes. I grappled over multiple rocks and there were even small wooden ladders at two or three different spots to help navigate over the larger boulders. We walked by a few caves where I could see bats flying around, but luckily we walked by and not through those caves.

This whole time, Fernanda was not talking at all. Almost the entire hike, which was close to two hours, she said maybe ten words, and most were in Spanish. On Airbnb, it stated that it would be a bilingual tour and guides spoke English. That was incorrect. She didn't speak any English and didn't understand much English either.

We got to the first waterfall/cave and she just said, "Selfie?" "Uh no, I'm good thanks," I replied. We got to a place where we'd have to swim through a cave to get to another waterfall. I'm not exactly sure what she said, but I heard the word *ropa*. Since I was wearing my bathing suit under my clothes, I think she was asking me if I wanted to take my outer clothes off. I have read where the current of the water can take off bikinis, so I thought it would be best to keep the clothes on.

We swam a very short distance and the water was maybe ten feet deep. It was a crystal, turquoise blue colored water. On the other side of the rock was an opening to another stream that was open overhead. As you swim toward that side, the sun just shines off the water, almost giving it a glowing effect. Quite astonishing.

She asked about a selfie again and I politely said no. It was starting to get a little awkward. I was really hoping to learn more about the area. It is near the Rincon de la Vieja volcano, which I believe is what makes the water that color. Rio Celeste also has a similar color. We did a little more climbing and we got to a large collection of water in between two very large cliffs. I saw two ropes going over the water through the narrow opening between the cliffs.

Fernanda looked at me and said, "Swim with ropes." Okie dokie. I had read in blog posts as well that the current is very strong at this point and this is where people can tend to lose their clothes. As I started into the water, I got about a quarter of the way in and I could already start to feel the current. I can see now why they want people to have guides. This could be very dangerous. Even though I was wearing workout shorts, the current was literally taking my shorts and my bikini bottoms off. I had to hold on a few times to make sure I kept my bottoms with me! I even struggled a bit to get up onto the rock, because I felt the current kept pulling me down.

Once I got up on the rock and went around the corner, I saw La Leona. It is a very beautiful waterfall that comes out of a small opening through one of the cliffs. It was obviously very strong due to all the rain that we had recently. The side of the wall where the waterfall falls down has a perfect concave area for the waterfall. The water wasn't warm, but it wasn't freezing. We'll go with refreshing, lol. There were a few other Americans who were swimming in the small pool. Fernanda went and sat on a rock by the wall. I took a few pictures and then asked if she was ready in Spanish. She said, "No swim?" I replied, "No," while shaking my head.

At this point, it was so uncomfortable, that I just wanted to be done with the hike. It's one thing when you're hiking by yourself, it can be peaceful and tranquil. When there is another person with you and they are almost completely silent, it just feels weird. Once we got to the top of the trail, she told me in Spanish that we had to walk to the entrance on our own, no ride. Great.

Fortunately, it wasn't too far, but it was really hot that day. Once we got to the end, she told me, again in Spanish, that someone was coming to get us. At least, I think that is what she said. As I sat there waiting for the ride, I opened the dry bag. It didn't work. There was approximately an inch of water in the bottom of the bag, which my rental car key fob was floating in. Oh yay, perfect.

Luckily, the key fob still worked by the time we got back to the car. I gave the dry bag to Fernanda and asked for Jonathan. She said that he wasn't there anymore, but I could call. She kind of stood there and looked at me for a minute. I'm not sure if she was waiting on a tip or what, because she didn't say anything ... again. I collected my things from my trunk to change and told her thank you.

I contacted Jonathan and told him what happened. He apologized and issued me a refund right away. He said that he had over 350 guests and never had that complaint before. For the fact that she doesn't speak, but maybe ten words of English if that, I kind of doubt that statement, but whatever. The waterfall was beautiful, the hike was challenging, but in a great way. I would recommend it to others but with a different tour company. Do not use the one on Airbnb.

Days 6-10: The Search for Good Food, Sunsets, and a Clean Mouth

As I said, there are quite a few restaurants in Coco Beach. The typical sodas were a little pricier than Fortuna and not as good. There were more bars, especially touristy bars like Coconutz. The food was still decent and I liked the swing chairs, but still a tourist trap nonetheless. Some of my favorite places were off the beaten path.

Restaurante Mar Azul was at the top of my list when it came to restaurants. Not only was it a five minute walk from my condo, but the fish was always fresh and inexpensive for the amount you got. My favorite appetizer there was carpaccio, which I got to try bluefin tuna, white marlin, and octopus. All incredible and 100 percent delicious! The sashimi itself was very fresh and they had homemade sauces that complimented the fish perfectly. They always gave complimentary pumpkin cream soup, which was so savory, but light and creamy at the same time. The main entree that people came for was where you can get almost any fish made to order. You choose the fish, whether you want it grilled, fried, blackened, etc., then the sauce and sides. I tried the whole snapper and also bluefin tuna. It was less than twenty dollars. Great value with outstanding flavor!

The sunsets are spectacular here and many places have happy hour so that you can enjoy cheap drinks while relaxing and admiring the sunset. On my first night, I walked to Café de Playa, which was a restaurant on the property of a beachfront hotel off of the main strip. The cafe has a large patio that leads directly up to the ocean while serving great drinks at a great price every day from 4-6 pm. A perfect way to end a day.

The Lookout was another good restaurant but was much more expensive. The view was great, especially for sunsets. I made a turn off the main strip exiting Coco. Then I went through a residential area and up many windy and narrow roads before reaching the restaurant. Their website, unfortunately, like many others within Costa Rica, does not have updated information. It still says happy hour all over its website, including Facebook and Instagram. I arrived and they said no more happy hour due to Covid. They said that they hadn't had it in months. They did offer me a complimentary shooter called a Chiliguaro, which has cacique, lemon, Tabasco, salt, and pepper. It wasn't too bad, but didn't make up for the lack of happy hour, because their menu items are pricey otherwise.

Hot Wok was another restaurant that hadn't updated its website. They had a Sunday buffet for years, but stopped it, also due to Covid. They also had a huge banner in front of their restaurant still advertising the buffet. I totally get that things had to change due to Covid, but it only takes a small bit of time to update certain things on a website. I am anything but tech savvy, especially with websites, but I know that it only takes a few minutes to take down a happy hour or buffet information. It only takes fifteen minutes to take down a banner.

People still came for those things, some out of the way from where they were, only to be disappointed and left with the choice of staying, paying more money, or looking for another place at the last minute. I'm sure Costa Rica isn't the only place that is doing this, but I definitely noticed a strong pattern.

Another positive note of this town is its medical care. I didn't really need to have much done during my stay, but I did come across Dental Tourism. I didn't even know that it was a thing until I was getting desperate to get a deep cleaning performed on my teeth. So many places in Vegas and even my hometown in Mooresville, NC just completely rip you off with the pricing. Some places were charging close to eight hundred to a thousand dollars for the procedure. After doing research, I found a clinic in Coco before I even arrived. LS Dental Clinic is a wonderful office that was less than a five minute drive away from my condo. Dr. Stephanie was absolutely fantastic. For the first time in years, I actually felt like a dentist was telling me the truth and not trying to rip me off. She said that a deep cleaning in the US is their regular cleaning there in Costa Rica due to more professional and deeper laser cleaning. Not sure if that was true, but it was a very thorough cleaning and it only cost me sixty dollars! She even scheduled for me to come back in two weeks to follow up for free. I would recommend this office to anyone! I wish I could come back every six months just for them.

Playas del Coco really does have welcoming and kind locals, great food, and a spectacular beach. It's the perfect place to have as a home base for holidays or even as an expat. Highly recommended!

Days 11-15: All-Inclusive Birthday Weekend

My forty-first birthday fell within my trip to Costa Rica. My fortieth was somewhat of a bust thanks to Covid (thanks Covid!) so I wanted a "birthday redo" of sorts and decided to book a weekend getaway for myself. On my first trip to Costa Rica, I was not alone and we stayed at an all-inclusive resort within Guanacaste. I did some research and I found another all-inclusive resort that was only a fifteen-minute drive from Coco Beach and my Airbnb. I had found a deal at the Marriott El Mangroove Hotel and Spa in Papagayo, Guanacaste that was all-inclusive of food, drinks, AND spa treatments. I was so excited about unlimited spa treatments! When it came close to that weekend, I emailed ahead of time to make appointments for the spa. To my disappointment, the spa was not offering facials due to Covid, even though it wasn't listed on their website. Other than body scrubs and massages, their menu was a little limited. I booked myself a coffee detoxifying scrub and a deep tissue massage for the first day and then a volcanic soothing scrub with a tropical body polish on the second day.

They said that I could come early to start the unlimited spa treatments, but failed to mention that all-inclusive still didn't start until 3 pm. I wasn't informed until I arrived hungry and thirsty before my first spa appointment. After speaking with management, they gave me a complimentary drink and lunch in the spa while I waited for my treatment. It did take over an hour to get the food and drink, so I had to eat in a hurry. There weren't many people at the spa and it felt like I had the place to myself. All of the spa treatments were lovely and well worth the visit.

On the first night, I struggled to get drinks at the bar and most of the food that I tried to order was not on the all-inclusive part of the menu. Argh. At one point, I waited at the bar, alone, for over twenty minutes and all of the bartenders ignored me. A couple walked up to the bar and they waited on them right away. Well, if that doesn't suck. I ended up going to a server to ask for a drink. It can already be difficult and mentally draining being a solo traveler, but when it seems that people are ignoring you because you are alone, it feels pretty defeating and frustrating.

The next day, one of the managers asked how things were going. I told them what happened and things changed quickly after that. The service manager even came out to apologize and made a drink for me himself. The breakfast staff was probably the nicest out of all the staff. One of my servers even created a special thing for my birthday and brought it out to me. A group of them sang and brought me a glass of champagne. It can always be hard to celebrate your birthday alone, but with people like this, it sure makes things a lot easier.

The resort also offered a free rental for water sports activities. I had never tried stand-up paddleboarding yet and it was on my list of things to try. One of the guys gave me tips on what to do, but couldn't give me a "lesson" without payment. I went on my own out into the ocean and it was wonderful! I was too chicken to stand up, but I did get to half kneeling. The water was a gorgeous and clear blue that was calm from being in a cove. You almost felt like you were in a lake instead of the ocean with how calm the water was. They had a pirate ship in the middle of the cove that you could paddle around. It was so much fun and relaxing at the same time.

Overall, the trip was good and I'm glad I did the getaway. El Mangroove was not my favorite and I wouldn't stay there again nor would I recommend it. For some of the things that happened there, even things that I didn't mention, there are too many resorts in that area for that kind of service for that high of a price.

A few days after my birthday, I made arrangements to drive down to Samara Beach. Time to explore more of the Costa Rican coast!

Samara Beach

Days 1-3: We're Not in Coco Beach Anymore, Toto

During my stay in the Guanacaste region, I wanted to check out a few more beaches and explore more of the country's coastline. I would go to a city for one to three days, then head back to Coco. It was so nice having a home base. My first trip outside of Coco Beach was to Samara Beach. I'll start by saying that I was very excited about coming to this beach, because of all the wonderful reviews that I had read throughout the net and the CR groups that I was a part of on FB. I was sadly disappointed. Majorly.

Full disclosure here: I did not have many positive experiences in Samara, except for a beach and one or two restaurants. I just wanted to give a heads-up that this chapter may have a negative tone or connotation.

I knew before going that Samara was an underdeveloped town and there wasn't much there. For the record, I have no problem with this. I grew up with my vacation home as a child being at a small beach in southern NC, which was underdeveloped in the '80s into the '90s. I have no problems with small, underdeveloped towns. In fact, I actually enjoy them. They typically have more charm and you have this feeling that you have the place to yourself.

The beach was very pretty. You could tell that it hadn't been too disturbed by tourists or developments. Half the beach had a white, sandy, squishy-under-your-toes appearance. The other half was almost all pebbles, which made it difficult to walk or lay on. It's interesting how the beach can have two completely different surfaces, but there isn't anything noticeable that is actually dividing the beach. The water was a mix of colors and shifted from a deep blue to a light turquoise color. It was quite gorgeous. There were signs everywhere that warned swimmers and surfers about the rip current. You can tell by the waves that the current is rougher than Playas del Coco or some other beaches. It is a place that surfers really love.

So what was I disappointed with? It definitely wasn't the beach itself. For the most part, it was the people of Samara. I experienced horrible customer service at almost every place that I walked into.

I walked into Roots Bakery, which was ranked very high on Tripadvisor and other websites. There was a line, which is usually a good sign, but it could have been because there aren't very many places to go for a quick pastry and coffee. The cashier spoke English, but I tried to speak Spanish like I have since I arrived in CR. I ordered my coffee and then I asked how much two different pastries were. After she told me the price for each pastry I said that I would like both in Spanish. I said, "Los dos." Of course, there can always be difficulty hearing people when trying to hear someone through a mask, but she didn't ask for clarification and she didn't read off my order. When I heard the total, I felt that it was a bit high, but I had already handed her my credit card. When I got the receipt, I realized that she charged me for two of each pastry. I don't know if she just heard "dos" or two, but it still wouldn't make sense to me; two of what?

I immediately went back to the counter when I saw the error. She said there was nothing that she could do. Excuse me? What do you mean that there is nothing that you can do? A tall, young gentleman who seemed like a manager came up and the lady told him what happened. He told me that once a transaction goes through, there was nothing that could be done. Oh, hold up! I looked at him and called bullstuff. I mentioned to him that every POS system has a way of reversing a transaction, especially since there weren't any other orders that had gone through the system after mine. Even then, if for some strange reason, it couldn't be reversed, he could have given the difference in cash, but he was trying not to. It made me wonder how many people don't even look at their receipts and what they are charging other people. Neither one of them talked to me and I saw both of them at the POS.

After a few moments, the lady looked at me and gave me a new total, and asked for my card. I gave her my card and she gave me a new receipt. She didn't say anything else. I asked her about the first transaction and she said she canceled out of the system. Oh! It can be done, I thought to myself sarcastically. I asked her about the receipt. She gave me an eat shit and die look. I gave her one back. She asked the gentleman and he helped her print off the cancellation receipt.

I just stood there wondering why that had to be so hard. As the day went by and I did more research about the town and what other places they offered, I realized that I might be left to go back for coffee again in the am. Sure enough, I was back the next morning. A different lady was at the cash register this time. All I ordered was coffee to go. I noticed on both days that they charged me more than what was written on the menu on the wall. I didn't say anything. After she gave me back my card, she wasn't going to give me a receipt. I asked her for one and again her facial expression looked like I was asking her for a kidney. Not really sure what that is all about. If you visit Samara and need coffee, I'm sure you will be going to this place. Make sure you ask for a receipt and really look it over.

One day, I was laying on the beach and I got thirsty and decided to walk over to Gusto Beach. I laid in one of their chaise lounge beach chairs, which said on signs that you needed to be a customer. There were two other women lying next to me in chairs and two different servers came up to them multiple times. I laid there for over an hour and no one came up to me. No one even looked at me or acknowledged me. Maybe I looked broke, who knows, lol.

Part of the bad customer service is mostly greed. I'm not sure if that is really counted as customer service, but restaurants and tour companies are so greedy. To be honest, many tour companies in CR do not like solo travelers. I was able to get a tour for kayaking as a solo traveler in La Fortuna. In Samara, I couldn't get most tour companies to even respond to me. There were two that responded. Outback said that they needed a three-person minimum. Three people! I'm used to hearing two people, but three?! I know times were rough, but wouldn't you want some money rather than none, especially if you have other people already on the tour? I've even seen online that places want to charge a solo traveler the same price as if there were two people. Dang. Troubles for solo travelers is a topic for another book.

The other tour company wouldn't provide transportation to Ostional Refuge for the Arribada (Turtle Nesting). That doesn't sound horrible until you find out that the roads to Ostional are currently so bad, that it takes a 4×4 or a specialized vehicle to get there.

Another part of the greed is how much restaurants are charging. Almost all of the restaurants charged more than any other place that I had been to so far in CR and the quality didn't match up to the price. The restaurants were even higher than in Playas del Coco, which is a more touristy and developed beachy town. There weren't many retail shops in town, but the ones I saw seemed of lower quality, but again with a higher price tag.

Since I couldn't get to Ostional Refuge, I did more research and saw that Camaronal Beach is closer, easier to travel to, and night tours with guides are cheaper. I found a restaurant in Playa Carrillo called El Colbri Restaurante, which was close to the beach. Wonderful experience. The staff was nice and had an absolutely fantastic ribeye at a reasonable price. I had the ten ounce ribeye and a glass of wine for twenty-nine dollars after tax and tip.

I got to the beach right before sunset in order to get a good viewing spot. I got lost trying to find the beach twice because Google Maps was giving the wrong directions. It was actually telling me to walk into the ocean to find the beach. Sigh. Right after 6 pm, the Rangers came out and shooed everyone off the beach. Someone who I was sitting close to, who spoke more Spanish than me, asked the Rangers about night tours. The Rangers told them that there weren't any. What? I literally looked at multiple websites, even *Tico Times* had written an article about it two weeks before.

As I started up my car, I saw two large tour buses pull up and a bunch of people get out. I turned off my car and got out. I asked the Rangers how there are no night tours if all of those people were walking in. The Rangers called an American male over to talk to me. He was the leader of the volunteer group that got off the tour buses.

He was on a power trip and gave me false information. He said that there weren't any night tours because of Covid. Seriously, I don't think turtles can get Covid. He tried to say that the police would fine everyone that would be out on the beach. If he volunteered for this organization and was knowledgeable about the area, he would know that Camaronal and Ostional were still giving night tours without police interference. I was getting so mad, especially with his condescending tone. I wasted the trip out there. The next day, I found out that multiple tour companies go there nightly, but I couldn't find them in time. Sigh.

The next day, I decided to go back to Playa Carrillo, because I saw a beautiful sunset on the way back to Samara that night. When I got there, there were tons of Ticos having BBQs, playing music, and enjoying time with their families. This felt like more of a local beach, which had a great feel. I didn't see many pebbles on the beach. It was nice and white. If anyone is in the Samara area, I would definitely recommend Playa Carrillo over Samara.

I had such a bitter taste in my mouth about Samara, I decided to leave a day early. I enjoyed Playas del Coco so much more and didn't need to torture myself and stay another day. On my way out, I tried to stop by Belen Waterfall, which isn't too far off the main road. It wasn't clearly marked and of course, Google Maps took me to the wrong place again. At one point, as I was traveling down the road, a farmer was leading his cattle from one part of the farm to another, but they had to use the road. I had to stay parked in the road for several minutes as the cattle made their way down the gravel road.

Once I found my way, I walked down a gravel/dirt road while hearing the water rushing through in the background. When I got to the bottom, I saw a handmade sign with words written in marker or crayon "$2 for visitors." I don't think this is even private property and I didn't see anyone around. I was literally the only person standing there. I could see the falls from the top. It looked like a steep, but short five minute walk to the falls. There was a lot of water and it was very brown from all the rain that had fallen lately. I felt that it wasn't worth walking down and paying two dollars for. I have heard that it is very pretty during the dry season. I could totally see that being true when the water is a little clearer. Maybe next time.

Flamingo and Tamarindo

Day Trip: Lifestyles of the Rich and Shameless

A week after Samara, I decided to do a day trip to Flamingo and Tamarindo. Flamingo Beach is less than an hour drive from Coco and Tamarindo is only thirty minutes past Flamingo; a relatively easy drive for a day. I tried to keep this chapter relatively short. One reason is because it was only a day trip. The other reason is that this chapter is, unfortunately, similar to the last chapter, Samara Beach. I did not have a great experience that day, but wanted to write about my experience so that others can be warned and stay cautious when dining alone.

I will start out by explaining why I decided to visit these places. During my first trip to Costa Rica, in 2013, I had a chance to visit Flamingo and Tamarindo, briefly. I had fond memories of both places. I recall getting a taxi from our all-inclusive resort in order to do some souvenir shopping and checking out Tamarindo's sunset. This was recommended by the staff at the resort. The souvenirs were cheaper than the resort and we were able to catch a cheap meal in town. We sat in the sand amongst tourists and locals alike as we watched the sun set behind the ocean. It was one of the most beautiful sunsets that I had ever seen. The sky was a vivid blood orange color with highlights of yellow and orange sherbet hues around the sun. Along with the deep, royal blue color of the sea, it was absolutely gorgeous. My pictures came out so well, I have one of the pictures on an aluminum canvas in my room to this day. One could say that my expectations were high because of these memories.

My first stop was Flamingo Beach to lay out in the sun for a bit. I knew I wanted to eat in Tamarindo later. As I approached the town, I noticed that the beach itself was pretty small and it didn't seem very developed for such a luxurious and popular beach. I was able to find the beach without too much trouble. Parking was a little scarce and people mostly parked along the side of the road. I saw one or two restaurants across from the beach and a few luxury resorts beachfront.

As for the beach itself, if you are looking for a white sandy beach with lighter blue water, this is your place! It had some of the softest and whitest sand that I saw in Costa Rica, other than Manuel Antonio Beach.

The beach, stores, and restaurants are considered more upscale and attract more of the "upscale and bougie" clientele. I didn't see much nightlife, so it seemed that it might be more for people who are there just for the beach and do not leave their resort, which is totally fine. Everything seemed much more expensive than some of the surrounding areas. For me, it was a good place to visit for the day when I wanted to lie on a nice beach for a few hours.

After Flamingo, I headed to Tamarindo to grab a late lunch and hopefully scope out a happy hour or three. Tamarindo is known for being very touristy and extremely crowded. That was definitely the case on the day that I visited, which was a Thursday. It was the most crowded that I have seen in any town that I have been to in Costa Rica. So many people walking along the streets, going in and out of shops, and restaurants were packed.

I was really craving sushi and read about a place with really good reviews called Wabi Sabi. Oddly enough, there was no one in this restaurant. The rolls were pretty good, mostly average, but very expensive. It didn't really seem like the price was worth what you get. I also thought it was strange that they didn't have any sort of cocktail/beverage menu. When I tried to ask the waiter, he wanted me to tell him specifically what drink I wanted. An indecisive person needs choices! Lol. It was also the first sushi place that I've been to that didn't have sake. I think all of that might be the reason that I was the only one in there. Maybe just not a great first impression.

After lunch, I walked around the main strip looking for happy hour. There were many stores, souvenir and clothing stores alike. Prices were a little higher than in other places, but not by much from what I could tell.

I found a small bar a few feet off the main strip called Wild Panda. They had two for one drinks and I tried their red sangria. The bartender's name was Mike and he was a charming, middle-aged guy that looked like he belonged in a movie as Javier Bardem's double. He made the sangria sooo strong, but sooo good. He spoke very good English and even waved into my phone when I was on Facetime to say hello!

After happy hour, I decided to walk along the beach to try and find a good spot to watch the sunset. I found a beachfront restaurant that served happy hour for the sunset, El Chiringuito. I waited for a table to clear and they sat me along the front row on the beach. This place also advertised two for one drinks. I ordered a glass of white wine, which can be difficult to drink when it's hot because it gets so warm so quickly out there. I ordered two glasses of wine and a tuna poke bowl. The bowl was decent, but nothing spectacular. The sunset came and went. It was about as magnificent as I remembered, and I had the perfect view. It was then time for the bill.

The server tried to take my card before I saw the bill, but I was able to ask for the bill first. As I looked over the bill, I noticed that I was charged for two glasses of wine and not the advertised special. I asked the server about it and he said, "Oh, we gave you two pours into one glass." Uh, what?? So, you're saying that you have given me four glasses of wine?!" I frustratingly replied. I wasn't quite finished with the second glass, but it had gotten warm and I gave up on it. The glasses were quite big and the pour looked relatively heavy, but not two full glasses worth. There was also nothing on the menu that said that two drinks would be in one glass. As I looked around, I noticed that everyone's liquor drinks looked normal, nothing large. I asked why he didn't tell me that there were two glasses poured into one beforehand because I wouldn't have ordered another one otherwise. He just shrugged his shoulders. I could tell that I was being scammed or they were at least attempting to. "May I speak to the manager?" I asked. The manager came right over and said, "Oh sorry, all good. We will take the second glass off." I said, "Ok, I'm going to the restroom as you fix the bill." The manager nodded.

After leaving the restroom, I stood next to the bar/kitchen and waited for my bill. My server and manager just walked past and ignored me for over twenty minutes. I kept trying to get someone's attention, but I kept being ignored. I finally just left the money in cash on the bar. Needless to say, I won't be back and wouldn't recommend this place to others. There are way too many other places on this beach for that mess.

Other than Samara, Tamarindo was one of my least favorite places to stay in Costa Rica. I felt that it was more of the armpit of Costa Rica than Jaco, which is what Jaco is known for. Jaco is another story for another time. I do try to avoid driving there in the dark because there aren't street lights, the roads are crazy, and drivers can be even crazier. I left Tamarindo around 7:30 pm and drove the one and a half hours back to Coco in the dark to call it a night. Hope my next few beach adventures will turn out better than today!

Jaco

Days 1-3: Armpit of Costa Rica? I Don't Think So...

I started out my ten-day journey on the southern coastline. Jaco was 134 miles away from Coco and it took about four hours to drive. Halfway, I decided to stop for a hike that was recommended by a local in Fortuna. Cerro Pelado is off the main highway, along more windy and narrow roads. It's a common theme in Costa Rica, if you haven't noticed from my stories so far. Google Maps took me the wrong way again and I lost about an hour or so of my time driving. Cerro Pelado is an extinct volcano where you can hike to the top. It is very majestic, green, and a wonder. The hike is moderate with the trail being quite uneven and rocky. I was able to climb almost eight hundred feet in less than thirty minutes. Once up at the top, I saw the Cerro Pelado sign. Off to the right, I also saw a small hill with a rubber tire staircase with a rubber rope railing. The railing is definitely needed due to the wind.

I mention the wind, because, holy crap, the wind up there is crazy! I used one of the bamboo sticks lended to me and I definitely needed it. Once at the top, I had to hold the stick with my arms and place it through my backpack so the stick wouldn't blow away! I took a video where I couldn't even hold the camera still. I believe that this mountain is called bare hill because the wind won't let anything grow.

The hills have a path through the rest of the small hills up to the peak. Some places have rubber railings and some places don't. Like most hikes that I have done in Costa Rica, I was completely alone up there. I was struggling with the wind and placing my feet on the ground. I started along the path and the moment that I slipped and the wind was taking me down, I won't lie, I totally became a chicken and couldn't finish the last little bit. It was a looong way down and there was no phone reception. I felt disappointed in myself that I couldn't complete it. Next time, I hope.

After the hike, I made my way down to Jaco. Jaco is one of the oldest, most developed beaches in Costa Rica. Many years ago, it was one of the nicest beaches, but now it is somewhat run-down in some people's opinions. I have heard many call it the armpit of the Costa Rican beaches.

I, on the other hand, disagree. I enjoyed the area. Was the actual beach the nicest? No, not really. It was a light to dark brown sand with a good bit of debris and a little trash here and there. The sand was only slightly sandy due to being mixed with small and medium pebbles. Not super comfortable to walk on when I was there. The water was not clear, but it also wasn't the darkest or murkiest water that I've ever seen. The waters are slightly rough, which makes it very popular with surfers.

The people were very nice. Some of the nicest people I met in Costa Rica were in Jaco. I met some locals, but definitely a large mix with Americans and tourists. It was the one city during my stay in Costa Rica where I heard just as much English as I did Spanish. You can tell that Jaco has a large expat population. I did notice that the American expats were of an older generation, especially older men.

I did have one weird encounter walking down the main street of Jaco. As I walked, I noticed a middle-aged woman heading toward me. As she got closer, she seemed like she was going to walk straight into me. We did the weird shuffle that people will do when trying to avoid walking into someone, but her shuffle seemed deliberate. She got right up in front of me and placed her hands at my lower abdomen and my crossbody purse which was also located at my lower abdomen level. She gave a giggle and said, "Oh, we're dancing." She finally got around me and kept giggling as she walked. It gave me the heebie-jeebies to where I spent the next few days looking for sage to burn in stores around Jaco. (Note, I didn't find any). More than likely, she was trying to get into my purse. Luckily, I had my Travelon travel purse that takes more than a few seconds to get into.

The restaurants were great, at least the ones that I chose. There is one main strip with probably close to one hundred restaurants. I was able to walk the main strip from one side to the next in under thirty minutes. Most of the restaurants had great prices, much lower than most of the parts of Costa Rica that I had visited. The fish and seafood were fresh and there were happy hours everywhere. Breakfast was also good and most served bottomless coffee with cups that were as big as your head! There are also many chain fast-food places as well if you need a quick bite on the go. I did have a KFC craving one night and the nuevo chicken sandwich was quite yummy!

Some of my favorite places were Ohana Sushi, Tapas y Bar, and Graffiti Restro. Graffiti is a little overpriced, but their coffee rub steak is pretty awesome. Ohana was perfectly priced. I ordered multiple tapas for such a small price. I tried everything from their poke bowls, to their sushi, to noodles. All wonderful! The sushi was very fresh and the sauces complemented the fish very well. Carpaccio was also fresh and they give an ample amount for the price. Their drinks were also on point. I had a strong, yet tasty sangria with a price to boot. It was in a large, almost fishbowl shaped wine glass for five dollars. As you can tell, I highly recommend the place!

For breakfast, Sunrise Breakfast Place was one of my favorites. Bottomless coffee, perfectly cooked eggs (at least for me), and moist, perfectly sweetened banana pancakes. The reviews online are mixed, but I had a good experience all the times I visited. The owner is from the States and was very nice and friendly.

On Saturday, there was a farmers market in the Jaco Walk Shopping Center, the center that Graffiti is located in, along with many other restaurants and cafes. The farmers market was nice to sit and people-watch. There was a DJ playing music, and vendors selling homemade goods, clothing, etc. It almost made you feel normal while still in the weird times of Covid.

Speaking of Saturdays, the nightlife was definitely hopping here, even with Covid. I can only imagine what it will be like once Covid is past us. The main strip was brightly lit with neon and lively with people at bars and along the streets. Some people complain that it can be too loud and rowdy, but I didn't feel that way. Now, that could be because it was off-season, Covid, or any number of things, but it didn't seem crazy to me. Myrtle Beach or Daytona in the States could easily take the rowdy prize over Jaco.

As far as adventures, there is quite a bit to do with ATV tours, animal sanctuaries, ziplines, horseback riding, and even day trips to Isla Tortuga. I did the Isla Tortuga day trip out of Montezuma, and it was half the price. I did notice that food is cheaper here in Jaco, but adventures are pricier than in most other places/towns.

I didn't do many adventures in Jaco. Honestly, I had done so many adventures in other places. The thing that I enjoyed most was just walking around, eating, and exploring, which can easily be done here.

If you have a car, I highly recommend going up to Villa Caletas Hotel for their sunset. On a hilltop, they have an open amphitheater that has glorious views and the pictures that I have seen will be frameable. I didn't find out about this place until after my visit, but it is on my list if I ever make it back to Jaco! So, don't be steered away just because others call Jaco the armpit of Costa Rica. Just remember, to each their own and this place might just be your own! Off to my next adventure!!

Montezuma Beach

Day One: My Boat Taxi to a Gorgeous Beach and Amazing Seafood Pasta

The day had come to go to Montezuma Beach. I made arrangements through Zuma Tours to do a boat taxi from Jaco to Montezuma (Mz). The tour company picked me up at my Airbnb promptly at the time that was emailed to me days before. I left my car at my Airbnb condo (the owners were nice enough to let me keep my car there for a few days). The van took me to the next beach over, Herrera Beach. This is a very small, but beautiful beach that only has a few condos and a large resort. The sand is whiter than Jaco and the water is much bluer and more crystal-like, while only being a fifteen-minute drive away. I always find it so interesting how much places can change with such short distances.

The boat arrived a few minutes late, but not too much. They let off the passengers from Mz that were visiting Jaco and then they piled our luggage on. The employees were nice enough to take out our luggage and place it safely on the boat. When you see the pictures, you notice that not too many more bags can fit on that boat! I think that there had to be at least fifty bags sitting at the front of the boat with one of the employees sitting at the nose of the boat to make sure that none of them flew away or bounced off. It was a full boat that could fit about thirty passengers. Again, I was one of the only solo travelers, so I took the single seat in the front of the boat.

The boat ride only lasted a little over an hour. It was a lovely ride. It was a speed boat, so definitely don't think we were pontooning it across the ocean and lounging. I did see a few people sleeping though. I don't think I could ever fall asleep on a speedboat. We were going pretty fast and it was difficult to take pictures or videos. The guides said to keep a lookout for dolphins and whales because it was the beginning of whale season. Sadly, we didn't see anything but water, but still a nice ride.

I would highly recommend doing a boat tour to get from one beach to another. Driving from Jaco to Mz would take anywhere from three to four hours and it was only eighty-two dollars for a round-trip ticket. I also recommend this company. I used them again later in Mz.

As we arrived at the beach, I was in awe. It was stunning. The tropical beaches that most people envision on postcards or on social media for Costa Rica and other tropical places: this is it. The sand was mostly white and soft. The water was a mix of crystal blue and a light emerald green, so clear that you can see the bottom of the ocean from quite a distance. The water was also very calm. Surfers would not be happy here. Mz has a reputation for attracting more "hippie" types of people, those who want to be one with nature and just chill and relax.

We deboarded the boat and luckily the walk to my hotel was five minutes. Almost anything in Mz is a five-minute walk. I believe that this town is the smallest I have seen in Costa Rica yet. It only has three streets, which form a zigzag pattern to connect to one another. I would say it has maybe two grocery/convenience stores and ten restaurants. I thought Samara was underdeveloped, but this is much smaller and even less developed. Wi-Fi is little to nonexistent throughout the town. At one point, I thought it was my hotel, but I soon found out that it was a city-wide thing. I think at one point I tested the Wi-Fi speed and it said 2 Mbps ... 2. Very difficult to do computer life and communication with only 2 Mbps. If it rains, just forget it. Put away all electronics, and sleep in a hammock with a mojito in your hand.

I decided to stay at El Sano Banano Hotel, a budget hotel in the middle of the city. They had a luxury sister resort called Liang Liang. While staying at El Sano Banano, you are able to visit Liang Liang and use their amenities, but it was a little further out of town and I didn't end up visiting. The hotel was clean and the staff was very friendly. The room was spacious and the air conditioning worked relatively well, but it was dark in the room. There wasn't much lighting anywhere in the room, including the bathroom. There was one window in the room and my bed was facing the window, where it was placed in a small corner up against the wall. Not enough light to brighten the room at night, but enough light to wake me up at sunrise. They had a lovely garden out back that was nice to walk through, but they had arranged tables in their restaurants for diners to enjoy the scenery. The indoor dining area was connected to the reception and had a tropical decor with wicker dining seats that had white coverings with a large green tropical leaf design.

After being in Costa Rica for so long, I started to adapt to having breakfast. So much so, that many times I was still full at lunch and ended up eating an early dinner. Since this town was so small, I tended to eat at the same place more than once if I liked it.

My first breakfast was at Cafe Artisanal. The waiter was nice, and service was a little slow, but the breakfast was decent and he made sure my coffee cup was always filled. My kind of guy! On the second visit, I was waited on by a different gentleman. He was not as nice or attentive. I was only able to get two cups of coffee and he charged me for two cups! Except for getting specialty lattes or iced coffee, I have never paid for a refill of drip-brewed coffee in Costa Rica. You typically get refills in the States, too. I commented to the guy that I wasn't charged per cup yesterday and he looked puzzled. I also commented that I hadn't paid for more than one cup of coffee in Costa Rica. He just rolled his eyes at me. I then replied, "It must just be you," and walked away. I didn't go back to that restaurant again.

I did, however, find a lovely gem that was beachfront by the rocks. The restaurant was called Cocolores. It was part of a hotel/resort that was located down by the ocean shore. I had some outstanding seafood pasta. The seafood was so fresh and had just the right touch of garlic. They also had some good wine that was reasonably priced compared to other places in Costa Rica with a spectacular view of the water. There were several solo travelers who would dine there. We would be in the seats at the table that were facing the ocean. We all just came for the great food, booze, and view. I went back to Cocolores a few times during my stay. Soda Típica Las Palmeras was another family-owned restaurant just outside of town close to the beach that I also recommend.

I also hit a couple of two for one happy hours at the local bars. I don't know why, but I just feel it's a little weird to have both drinks at the same time. I know it's not just a Costa Rica thing. I've had a select few places do the same thing in Vegas, but I just don't get it. Maybe I just don't drink fast enough, but my second drink is either watered down or hot by the time I finish my first drink.

Day Two: Snorkeling Isla Tortuga and a Coco Loco

The second day that I was in Mz, I signed up for a day trip to Isla Tortuga with Zuma Tours. We got on the same type of boat from the day before minus luggage, and the trip was a little over an hour. One of the guides stopped the boat every so often to point out ancient waterfalls or caves. We continued to look for whales and dolphins without any success. We arrived at Isla Tortuga and we got to go snorkeling at two different coves close to Tortuga. I'm not sure if it was the boat ride or salt water, but after the first snorkeling trip, I wasn't feeling too hot. I was worried that the fish might end up eating my breakfast … yuck. I ran into two more American women and they said they were feeling the same way. Glad it wasn't just me.

The first snorkeling excursion was cool. For the most part, I saw fish that I've seen in other warm water places. I did, however, get to spot a pufferfish. I was excited to see and get close to the fish. Obviously, I didn't get too close, but I would have liked to have seen the fish stick out its spikes just once. That may be weird, but I'm weird, so go with it!

The guides told us that there are usually sea urchins nearby, but we didn't get to see those either. I asked if we would we be able to eat them if we found some. I wasn't completely joking, but also not completely serious. I had a feeling that we couldn't, but that would be amazeballs if we could. Sea urchin is one of my favorite things to eat. The guide laughed a little and said that they were protected in the waters that we were in and couldn't touch them. Oh well, I guess I'll have to keep getting my live sea urchins at Redondo Beach in California.

The water at Isla Tortuga is clear and crystal blue. The beach was lovely, but a little small. We were sharing the beach with other tours and we weren't allowed to go to certain parts of the beach. They prepared lunch for us there on the island. It was simple, but actually quite flavorful and tasty. They grilled bluefin tuna that they caught earlier that morning, along with fresh veggies with beans and rice.

After lunch, we had a few hours to ourselves to swim, sunbathe, drink, whatever we chose to do on the Isla. I did try their signature drink, Coco Loco. It was rum, coconut cream, coconut water, lime, and a touch of pineapple juice. It was tasty, but also really strong. One was just enough for me. It was a relaxing day spent sunbathing and swimming, while chatting with a couple other American ladies, in the calmness of the cove. It would have been nice to have other activity options or more of the beach to be able to stroll.

There was one guide that was trying to be very friendly and practice Spanish with me. Even without his mask, his accent was so strong and different, that I just struggled to understand any of his Spanish, which left me a little embarrassed and feeling stupid. There were two other women walking around, who obviously spoke better Spanish than me and were interpreting for him. To go through all that, we may have well kept speaking English to each other lol.

Tortuga was the first and only time I tried one of Costa Rica's beers, Silver Imperial. When you are super hot on a beach, a cold beer sounds way better than water. It was also included in the tour. It wasn't the best beer that I ever had, but it still beats a PBR and cooled me off a bit.

I highly recommend this tour with this company. It's a great way to spend a day when you can eat, swim, and relax!

Day Three: Three Waterfalls, a Crash Course in Rock Climbing, and a Staredown with a Monkey

On my last day, I decided to do the Montezuma Waterfall hike. It has three waterfalls, plus a hidden waterfall that you have to know about ahead of time or have a guide with you. The entrance to the falls is only a ten to fifteen minute walk from the center of town. At the entrance, there is a basic and simple map that explains the different waterfalls and trails. It also had the trails labeled between easy, moderate, and severe. They do recommend having a guide with you because there is not really any signage that tells you where the trails are. The trail was not paved or cleared out to where you could really see a definitive trail or path. You also have to go through the creek/river a few times to stay on the trail.

There are men that stand along the trail close to the entrance that will give you a few clues and then try to get you to hire them as a guide. I decided to go it alone, as usual. I did see more people along this trail than I have on any trail that I've done so far in Costa Rica, so I figured I would be good. The guide did give me a tip: in the first third of the trail or so, you will see where people have sprayed orange paint on different rocks and trees. This will signal what direction to go.

I made my way through the creek and along the embankment. I saw a couple of people above me. Not really sure how I missed that trail, but I was able to climb up to the trail to continue on toward the first waterfall, which is actually the largest. The last few feet before reaching the waterfall, there was no trail and not really even much ground to walk on. There were large rocks along the embankment and I could see where people had tied multiple ropes together across the rocks to get to the other side. So, there I went. I am always very klutzy and know how I tend to fall hiking, so I went even slower than normal and was very nervous. I'm always afraid of falling when hiking, because the last thing I would want is to get injured while traveling outside my home country. I'm also afraid of falling, because if I get injured, how will I get off the trail on my own? I have never really done any sort of rock climbing and I haven't done much rock rappelling either. You've got to start somewhere, right?

As I got closer, I saw off to the left-hand side of the river a sign that said "Waterfall 1 and 2". I knew I would need to figure out how to get over there later. I finally made it to the third waterfall. It was quite beautiful and was coming off to the side of the mountain/cliff. There was a moderate size pool to swim in, which many people were in, since it was hot and humid that day, like most days in Costa Rica. I saw toward the back that there was more water. It was the trickling of water from the first and second waterfalls above. I then saw what looked like a hidden trail. It looked very steep and there were multiple ropes, because I think you almost had to pull yourself up the trail. There was a couple standing there taking pictures of it. They told me that was the severe trail that led up to the rest of the waterfalls, but it was really dangerous. You could see signs around that said dangerous, but I'm sure many people still took their chances from time to time.

Among the people, there was a young guy that I met the first night in town. Many called him the town kook. He had been in town for a couple of months and took people on a "walking tour" through the city, inviting newcomers to come along with him. He liked to tell the story of how he was a marine biologist and speaks seven languages. Some people say that he tried to get money out of them for some new business. Fortunately, I never got a chance to hear that pitch. He was at the first waterfall giving people tips on how to get to the other ones.

I decided that it was time for me to try and head to the other waterfalls. I found a place in the river that was relatively low and crossed over and up to the next trail. This trail was much more well developed with mostly steps and handrails. It was steep and I had to take a few breaks to catch my breath. During this journey, my physique and overall health improved immensely, but stair climbing still kicks my butt. Along the way, I ran into an American woman, Kathy, and her local guide, Carlos. Carlos liked to mention that he is the top-rated guide in Mz. Now, there definitely could be only five guides in this town, but I do give him props for being number one. As we continued up the steps, all three of us continued talking and somehow I ended up being adopted into this small tour. We got to the first and second waterfall and as I took pictures, Kathy and Carlos decided to wait for me, which was really nice of them.

When first coming off the trail, the first waterfall is to the right, a hidden one to the left. To see the second, you have to either jump down off the first waterfall or climb down the rocks. Kathy and Carlos decided to jump, but I decided on the rocks route. I really didn't bring things to jump into the water, including something for the phone and camera. If you recall, I mentioned that I have never really done any rock climbing. Well, it was time for my crash course. It was about a fifteen-foot drop from the top of the waterfall down to the bottom. There also wasn't any ground for a few feet. There were more ropes that were used to get yourself over the rocks. For some reason, I was really struggling trying to figure out how to get down and where to put my feet.

Here comes the kook.

Somehow, he had climbed up all the other waterfalls from the bottom one and was down below me. He was kind enough to try and help me across the rocks. His advice wasn't any good, but he did end up physically helping me in the end, which was awesome. I took a couple of pictures and it was time to climb back up. I wasn't as nervous to climb back up as I was to go down, but Carlos was standing there waiting for me. He climbed down to where I was and gave me step-by-step instructions on where to put my feet.

Carlos then took Kathy and I to the hidden waterfall, but we didn't stay long, only long enough to take a few pics. Carlos then led us up the trail toward the back of the trails. We ended up at the top of a hill on the opposite side of where the entrance was. I thanked them for allowing me to be a part of their group for the day. Carlos never asked me for money, but I did give him some for his kindness and for being somewhat of a guide for me that day as well.

As we were walking along a road down the hill, Kathy said, "Carlos, you still haven't produced any monkeys yet!" Carlos laughed and replied,

"I've tried, but they don't listen to me." Kathy then said to me, "I have been mentioning to Carlos for the last few days that I have to see monkeys before I go home."

"I wish you luck," I replied. "I've been here for six to seven weeks and I haven't seen hardly any." A few minutes later, we heard a noise coming from the trees. We stood still for a moment to try and figure out where the noise was coming from and what was causing it. We could hear leaves rustling and almost what sounded like a jumping noise nearby.

Sure enough, a family of white-faced monkeys was coming down through the trees and crossing the road. You could tell that they were somewhat used to humans because it seemed like they were waiting to get food from us. When we told them and showed them that we didn't have any food to give, they started yelling and screaming at us. Holy moly! Feisty little guys. I had one little guy show me his food hiding place as he was reaching his arm down into a tree trunk and pulling out something to put in his mouth. One monkey was at eye level with me and decided to have a staring contest. After a moment or two, I realized that I could potentially lose more than the staring contest, so I quickly walked away.

Carlos had us stop halfway down the hill at Butterfly Brewery. He said that it was his second home. We stopped and got a bite to eat, along with a beer. Butterfly Brewery is owned by an American who was born and raised in Seattle and moved to CR when he was twenty-three years old. I would say he's in his late thirties now. All the beers are micro-brewed there. All their sauces, including ranch, are made homemade there. Raaaancch! Omg, I haven't seen ranch in seven weeks! Sometimes it is just the little things that you miss from home that you don't know you would miss until you can't have any.

The food was tasty and the beer was even better. I would recommend this place to anyone, especially on your way down from hiking. They are cash only and didn't have any Wi-Fi. We found out that the reason why they didn't have Wi-Fi is because someone took out all the copper wiring for their phone and Wi-Fi systems a few months ago during quarantine. The things people do when they're desperate.

While we were eating and having a drink, we started talking to Carlos about where he came from and why he was there. He was born and raised in La Fortuna. He came to Mz for his wife and kids, but he is unfortunately divorced now. He spoke of the struggles everyone had here due to Covid, including himself who survives off of tourism.

It was just a lovely time with three strangers who came from different parts of the world and shared food, beer, and laughter.

I asked him what locals do when they're not working around here, especially since it was so small. He said that there were no "locals" that really lived in Mz. Most Ticans live in nearby towns and commute in for work. He said that most people here are American, European, or Canadian. The only things that they do during their time off are activities outdoors in nature or venture to the one or two bars that are in town for drinks.

Day Four: Off to Manuel Antonio, but What's That in the Water?!?!

Didn't do much that evening since I had to get up early in the am to go back to Jaco and drive to Manuel Antonio. I woke up early to pack and hopefully get breakfast. Apparently, the only breakfast place that is open before 7 am is Soda Artisanal, argh. I waited until 8 am for Sano Banano to open. I thought that the boat taxi said to arrive at 8:30 am and that I had plenty of time.

I arrived at the Zuma Tour office at around 8:21 am. There was a guy sitting out front and said my name. He said that they were waiting on me. Waiting on me? Wasn't I early? Well, when I got to the boat, there were quite a few people waiting out in the sand and looking at me. I looked at my email again and went oooops. The boat leaves at 8:30 am and we were supposed to have gotten there at 8 am. Crap! I'm rarely ever late and I felt bad, initially. We all got on the boat and left at 8:34 am. That isn't too bad, right? I think that it was perfect timing and that the other people weren't mad by the end of the boat trip. Let me tell you why.

About forty-five minutes into our hour-long boat ride, the boat started to slow down. Ooooh, that means they see something! I lifted up my head and there they were ... dolphins. Note I used the plural term. There was a whole family of dolphins that were swimming near our boat. At least ten at a time on one side. The boat stayed in that area for about ten minutes doing circles. The dolphins almost seemed like they were playing with us and were doing circles around the boat along with us. They were jumping in and out of the water and you could even see them swim under the water right next to the boat. Such a magnificent sight. Do you see why the other people might not be mad anymore? If I hadn't been a few minutes late, we could have possibly missed it. Everything happens for a reason, right? I think that was my first time seeing a dolphin. The fact that I didn't just see one, but I got to see so many was a very nice ending to a great time in Montezuma!

Manuel Antonio

Day One: Awesome Tarrazu Coffee and Scrumptious Grilled Octopus

A fter getting off my boat taxi in Jaco and getting to my rental car, I decided to grab breakfast in Jaco. I went back again to Sunrise Breakfast for my bottomless coffee and pancakes. At about this time, my stomach started feeling the effects of so many carbs and pancakes. I don't usually eat pancakes, but I started having a big craving while I was there, along with bread, cookies, and all the other carbs that I've been devouring. Luckily, my weight hasn't been affected due to walking and hiking so much, but I know I can't keep that up forever.

After breakfast, I headed out of Jaco. I stopped up at the top of the hill on the outskirts of town at the Mirador to take pictures. It is a place that I would recommend visiting for nice photos with a panoramic view of Jaco. There is also another place nearby called El Miro Mountain that has a colorful staircase with graffiti art and lovely scenery. I also didn't find out about this place until after my trip, but many pictures that I saw from friends who visited after have me recommending it as well.

The drive along the coast to Manuel Antonio is pretty easy since it's a straight shot with the usual passing of super slow cars with the occasional stoplight. Fortunately enough, my Airbnb was ready early and I stopped in Quepos to pick up the keys. I unpacked my luggage into the Airbnb and got the A/C running. Honestly, I know I run hot on most occasions, but I don't know how Ticans do it here without A/C. The humidity that builds up in these homes in such a small amount of time would be so hard for me.

It was a very cute home with two bedrooms that had open ceilings with just one roof above. I assumed that was to help with air circulation. There was a complete kitchen with a large coffee maker. The owner of the Airbnb was an aficionado of coffee. He was so kind as to drop off a bag of coffee that can only be found around that area that comes from Tarrazu. It was so yummy and a one pound bag was only around three dollars! The name of it is Cafe Quetzal. If you see any while you are there, I highly recommend trying some. If you could send me a bag, that would be great too lol!

After getting acquainted in the Airbnb, I was ready for an early dinner and maybe some happy hour drinks. I hadn't done much research on the area regarding restaurants like I normally do, but it didn't take long to find something since the town is so small. About three miles away was a highly-rated restaurant called Oceano Seafood. They were having a two for one happy hour, so I ordered some tasty margaritas. The food was absolutely amazing. The prices were a little high, but the service and the actual taste of the food made up for it. For an appetizer, I ordered the three types of crudo tuna. It was a large portion and could have been a dinner in itself. For my main entree, I ordered the grilled Spanish octopus. It was over twenty dollars, but it was a very large portion and just perfect. The octopus was perfectly grilled and had just the right amount of tenderness without being mushy. The mashed potatoes and the cream sauce drizzled on top complemented the octopus so nicely. It was also just as great the next day as leftovers!

Day Two: Rain, Rain Go Away and How Did I Miss the Beach?!

That night, I bought a ticket for the Manuel Antonio reserve park for the next day at 8 am. I was told that I should arrive early to beat the crowds, and the wildlife tends to be more active during the early morning.

I woke up to pouring rain. I had mentioned to the owner of the Airbnb that I was going that day and he said that it wouldn't be worth it because of visibility and also the mud. Unfortunately, my ticket was nonrefundable.

I waited until about 11 am to leave the house. It was still raining, but it had lightened up some. I decided to take my chances and make the drive out. I figured at least I could venture around the town, since I hadn't seen it yet.

I have heard many people speak highly of MA and they would say how they absolutely love it, but to be honest, I just can't see why. MA reminded me of a smaller version of Myrtle Beach, but dirtier. There was a small public beach, but no free parking. Everywhere I went, there were signs for paid parking and multiple people standing out front trying to persuade me to go in and pay. They become so persuasive that they turned from persuasive to aggressive. I had people actually walk out in front of my car to try and stop me. It was bad. I almost hit a guy that wouldn't move out of the way. That alone makes me like this town much less.

Somehow or other, I was able to find a free spot along an alleyway near a condo/hotel that was close to the entrance of the park. Getting into the park was easy and efficient. They checked temperatures and had sanitizer gel throughout. I had read mixed reviews about whether or not to use a guide. I was able to see some things without a guide, but I might have had a better experience with a guide with a scope to know exactly where animals are. I got the idea from others to somewhat follow groups that were looking at something and then see if you could see it. Didn't work too well for me, but it did for others.

I had overheard a group earlier say that they had seen a sloth with her baby and so I stood in the same area for at least fifteen minutes looking for the sloths. As I was looking unsuccessfully, a couple came up to me.

"Are you seeing anything?" the couple asked.

I replied with a sad voice while sticking my lower lip out, "No, I can't see what others had said that they saw."

"Well, did you see the sloth in the tree down over there across the bridge?" they asked.

"No, I don't think that I have walked down there yet," I replied.

"Come with us, we will show you where it is."

This couple was so nice they doubled back over to where they already had walked just to show me a sloth. My heart felt full at that moment, especially as I finally got to see a sloth that was having lunch on some leaves near the top of one of the tall trees of the forest.

There were these very bright and colorful crabs throughout the swamp area that were neat to look at. I could hear howler monkeys from afar like I normally do, but I still had yet to see one. Some said that they saw some white-faced monkeys, but they were gone by the time I got to that area.

I walked around for about four miles and decided to call it a day. I did see one small beach called Playa Las Gemelas, but somehow I missed the main beach. This is the beach that the whole town is known for. For some reason, I missed it in the research, that the most beautiful beach that everyone travels to see is actually in the park! You also can't see or access the beach without buying a park ticket every time. I never got to see the beach, because I wasn't about to spend another eighteen dollars just to hang out on the beach.

After the park, I was pretty hungry and found another restaurant that was highly rated. Falafel Bar is on the main street of MA and was also a wonderful find. I got the gyro plate that was about fifteen dollars and it came with sooo much! There was so much food, a free drink, and all the fixings that you could want. Onions, cabbage, peppers, cilantro, tons of sauces, etc. I am a sauce queen and I think I had like three or four different sauces on my plate, and even went back for more later. I also got a mango smoothie, which definitely hit the spot. The staff was wonderful and very attentive.

Later that night, I decided to drive to Quepos to get chocolates and more of that coffee to take back with me. On my way back, I saw a super cute farmers market by the marina that had music, food, cheese, and souvenirs right at dusk. It was a very pretty sight with the dark royal blue sky of dusk in the background with the low lights of the vendors' tents. Such a unique and spontaneous find.

Day Three: The Hidden Beach and What I Had Been Waiting for This Whole Trip!

The next day, I contemplated whether or not to head back to Coco early. I was a little bored and didn't really know what else to do. I did a little bit of research while drinking my yummy coffee and I came across a hidden beach that many locals go to. Well, that sounded perfect! As usual, I was looking to see what the locals really do, and how they live. It can be hard to figure this out since it feels, at times, that tourism can cover up what the Tican culture really is and what Costa Rica is really about.

I decided to head down to the hidden beach, called Playa Biesanz. I took a curvy road up a hillside to get there. Parking was along the side of the road and could be dangerous because the road was narrow and uneven along the shoulder. It could also be hard to spot. You had to do a little hiking in order to get to the beach, which was covered by trees and forest.

I parked my car on the road and as I got out, two squirrel monkeys were playing with one another by trees and power lines near my cars. It was cute watching them play with each other and occasionally stare at the people.

The trail was pretty rocky, uneven, and muddy. I would say that it was about half a mile to the beach. About halfway down, I started hearing howler monkeys. All of a sudden, I saw one of them jump from one tree to another going across the trail. I then saw that there were others. So surprising that it took until the end of my trip to finally see them! I have heard that it is rare to see them because they usually like to hide high in the trees. Soon after, I started seeing white-faced monkeys as well. Many different sizes, including babies just jumping from one tree to the next.

I couldn't believe how much wildlife I was seeing. I hadn't seen this much during my entire trip to Costa Rica. I spent so much money at different parks and sanctuaries to see all of this wildlife, when all I really needed to do was find an area like this. I finally reached the beach. It was a lovely, but small beach cove with an off-white sandy beach and blue water. There were beach chairs, kayaks, and snorkel rentals. Someone had brought a radio and was playing party music. You could tell that it was mostly locals and their families. It was crowded, but not overly packed. I started looking around the trees close to the beach, hoping to spot a sloth.

A nice man came up to me, I'm sure he could tell that I was looking for sloths or wildlife. He said to me, "Perezoso?" which is sloth in Spanish. I nodded my head. He pointed to a tree that was slightly hanging forward, shading the sand. He pointed out to me a sloth holding its baby. What a sight! Such a magical day being in the middle of this jungle with all this wildlife and a lovely beach.

The man ended up being the owner of one of the kayak rental places. He was friendly and talked with me for a bit about the area and asked where I was from. Later, he stopped by and offered a free kayak and snorkel when the crowd died down if I would like. I ended up not staying long enough, but it was a kind offer. As I was getting back to my car, the road had gotten crazy with people trying to find parking. I guess I arrived just at the right time. It was a struggle to get my car out and get turned around.

After I left the beach, I headed back to Quepos to grab lunch at the marina. The marina was quite modern. It had several restaurants and bars to choose from. Most were quite pricey, but I found one sports bar upstairs with reasonable prices. The food was just okay, nothing spectacular, but the view of the marina and the ocean more than made up for it.

The next day, it was time for me to head back to Coco. I stopped at Gaia Resort and had breakfast at the on-premise restaurant, La Luna. It was a great restaurant. Great coffee, juice, bread, fruit ... everything and the service was great! Another place I would recommend.

Even though I didn't really care for the town, I did however love almost all the food and coffee that I found. There are some great finds there and you don't have to look very hard, which is also a plus!

Reflections

After Manuel Antonio, I was only in Coco Beach for a few more days before flying back to the States. I had an awful experience with the American Airlines gate attendants at the Liberia Airport. Seems to be happening more and more nowadays. After this trip, I think this will be one of the last times that I fly with American if I can help it. The quality of service and staff with airlines has gone really downhill during Covid. I guess that statement can be applied across all industries. Hopefully, things will improve as Covid improves.

Covid did affect my trip, but nothing that was incredibly major. You couldn't tell if things were open or closed. You got used to washing your hands before entering stores and getting your temp taken. You could tell that many people were already beginning to lose their patience with wearing masks everywhere, especially in hot and humid areas. Other people would still judge you and could even sometimes make rude comments to you if you were not wearing a mask 24/7. Costa Rica is one of the more lenient countries for Covid restrictions, so it will be interesting to see what else I encounter throughout the rest of my travels.

I also learned to not put 100 percent faith in a map app on my phone. Google and Apple Maps both took me to the wrong place or on the wrong route on many occasions. The most memorable is still when Google wanted me to drive out into the middle of the ocean to get to my destination.

Another thing that took some getting accustomed to was putting toilet paper in the trash instead of flushing it. For those who are unfamiliar, Costa Rica has been intending to install a septic system capable of handling paper, similar to ones found in the United States, Europe, and other parts of the world, but has yet to do so. It took some getting used to remembering to put the paper in the trash. It eventually became second nature. So much so that it took me a few weeks to adjust once I returned home.

When I first visited Costa Rica years ago, I had a fantasy built up in my head about how wonderful this place is as a tropical paradise. Like many people that I have spoken with who have had the same idea: how great would it be to live here? Who wouldn't want to live in a tropical paradise, right? Being able to spend two months in this country allowed me to see the good, the bad, and the ugly. The experience popped my fantasy bubble. Don't get me wrong, Costa Rica is still a beautiful country with many beautiful people. I would still go back for smaller stays, but I can see how people can get lost in their fantasies about this country while being treated like kings and queens in their all-inclusive resorts.

What have I learned about myself so far? Ever since March 2020, when everyone's lives changed, one thing that I have learned has been about patience and flexibility. Am I an expert in either? Oh, hell no. Living and traveling through Covid has taught me to really try to go with the flow more because Covid taught us that we really don't have as much control as we thought we did. I'm used to having Wi-Fi work when I want it to and realized how dependent I am on it. Oh, I know, first-world problems. When trying to take care of your life in your country while being out of the country, you're going to need it. I also didn't realize until this trip that there are certain websites that will not let you have access if you are trying to access them outside of the US. I'll need to try a VPN on the next trip.

Most of the people that I encountered were very friendly and would give recommendations or suggestions without a second thought. I have had many ask me if I was ever lonely. To be honest, not really. I think much of this had to do with having a new relationship in the States and we were talking often throughout the day. I also conversed with my parents daily. Even though I knew I wasn't in "paradise" per se, I was in a better place than I had been for quite some time. I enjoyed my time alone while exploring the country. I knew the whole time that I was there, how blessed I was to be able to have this experience that most people can go through a whole lifetime and never experience. How could you get lonely with that?

I did meet people here and there along my travels to strike up conversations with. One thing that I noticed on this trip, it could be because of Covid, but many people would rather stay to themselves than be social. I, at times, was also one of those people. I think that it could have been the isolation that I had experienced for over a year now due to the shutdown. I got used to being alone and almost forgot how to socialize or sometimes even how to have a conversation. Some people were standoff-ish because they were afraid of catching Covid. I did become more careful and aware toward the end of the trip since I had to have a negative test just to get back into my own country. The last thing anyone wants is to be stuck in a foreign country unexpectedly without a place to stay. For those who really want to meet more people and socialize, I think joining group tours or staying in hostels are some of the best ways to meet people.

I also encountered many people who were surprised that I was alone and asked if I was ever scared. The only times that I ever experienced any fear was doing some of the hikes where I was completely alone. Well, at least the only human around. The times where I could hear bushes rustling, but not see what was causing the rustle definitely had me more aware of my surroundings and super alert. There was rarely a time that I would feel unsafe traveling through Costa Rica, other than driving at night, of course.

One bit of advice, be choosy about who you tell that you are alone. Try to read the person and the area around you. If you feel the heebie-jeebies and you are in the middle of the rainforest, tell them that your friend is around the corner. Your safety should always be your number one concern.

I also learned to face my fears and realized that I am stronger than I think I am. Grappling rocks and waterfalls? That wasn't me. Before this trip, I had never really done much hiking. I gained a new appreciation and love for it through this trip. My experiences here helped me to push harder than I would have if someone was with me. I even learned a new appreciation and love for myself. I have had many people approach me with surprise that I'm traveling solo, especially for a long period of time. People would tell me how brave or strong I was. I had never even seen it that way. I had never really seen it as a big deal, but as I reflect back, I can see how it can be intimidating and nerve-racking for some. I guess I have already forgotten about that scared little twenty-year-old in Spain.

This is one of my main reasons for writing this story and my other traveling journeys: to inspire. During my travels, I have had many people, mostly women, who have heard my story and told me that it inspires them—whether it is to travel solo for the first time or to keep going even when they haven't had such a great experience the first time around. I think that everyone should try at least one solo trip in their lifetime. It can really show you who you are as a person and what you are capable of. You can also see a different aspect or perspective when you don't have a companion to have tunnel vision with. Traveling solo really does test your strengths and weaknesses, and I look forward to seeing what more of myself comes out during my journey.

Packing List

I have had people ask me what I packed for my trip, which was a longer journey. Here is an example of some items that I recommend:

1. Clothing is very subjective, but I do encourage to pack as light as you can. If I can wash clothes in a sink, so can you. I do recommend black athletic socks; I have ruined many white pairs on my different trips.

2. Sunscreen - one of the most important things to bring. The sun is hotter here than you think, and it is almost double the price if not more if you buy it here.

3. Bug Spray - same as sunscreen.

4. Flashlight

5. Travel Aeropress for my coffee lovers

6. Wine corkscrew for my wine lovers

7. Folder with all important documents that have to be printed.

8. A secure crossbody purse - I recommend a crossbody messenger-style purse because you are able to keep it in front of you with your hands on it at all times. I carry a Travelon purse because it is built to stop theft. The fabric is hard to cut, there are latches on the zippers to keep things more secure, and even secret pockets that make a thief have to really dig through your purse to find valuables.

9. Travel insurance - you just never know, and most that I purchased cover medical if you got Covid.

10. TRX suspension cables - These came in really handy when I didn't have access to a gym. Note, these weigh about five pounds, which sucks when you are trying to keep your luggage weight down.

11. Selfie stick with gorilla tripod or similar with remote. I know this sounds silly, but solo travelers cannot always rely on someone else to take your photo and sometimes you want more than just your head in a picture lol.

12. Compression bags - These have always been my best friends. It has made packing much easier and it also helps with dirty or wet clothing.

13. Shoes – Keep it simple. Black and/or brown flip-flops, water shoes, hiking shoes, and regular sneakers. There are many Instagram influencers that carry around stilettos and cute high heels. I wear a size 10 shoe. Can you imagine how much room that takes up in a bag?

14. Apple Airtags - I have one in each of my pieces of luggage, including my carry-ons. Lately, airlines have been losing more

and more luggage and it is always good for your peace of mind knowing where your bag is located.

15. This trip I took my own pillow, but learned during my trips that taking my own pillowcase did just as well. For us older ladies who are worried about anti-aging, I made sure to have my satin case that was recommended. It also dries super quickly.

16. Portable battery charger - Map apps drain your phone battery like crazy, so I rarely leave home without mine now.

17. Universal adapter - This trip I had a large surge protector, but it broke easily and also was pretty heavy. Most of my electronics were dual-voltage, so I didn't really need to worry about converting.

18. Leave your hairdryer at home. Most places have them. I brought one curling iron and a straightener that was dual-voltage, but rarely used them. For people who have naturally curly or wavy hair, you will not really need any of these items in Costa Rica due to the humidity.

19. I carried a Tide to Go pen and travel-sized Downy Wrinkle Releaser, but both had leakage problems.

20. Ziploc bags - You just never know when you'll need a bag.

21. A lightweight day bag for hiking or just being out and about. I bought one that folded up into pocket size and it came in handy quite often.

Check out my Travel Store for links to the above and more recommendations at https://solotravelchronicles.com/travel-store/

Notes